RECOVERING

PASTORING FOR LIFE

Theological Wisdom for Ministering Well
Jason Byassee, Series Editor

Aging: Growing Old in Church
by Will Willimon

Birth: The Mystery of Being Born
by James C. Howell

Friendship: The Heart of Being Human
by Victor Lee Austin

*Recovering: From Brokenness and Addiction
to Blessedness and Community*
by Aaron White

RECOVERING

FROM BROKENNESS
AND ADDICTION

TO BLESSEDNESS
AND COMMUNITY

AARON WHITE

Baker Academic
a division of Baker Publishing Group
Grand Rapids, Michigan

© 2020 by Aaron White

Published by Baker Academic
a division of Baker Publishing Group
PO Box 6287, Grand Rapids, MI 49516-6287
www.bakeracademic.com

Library of Congress Cataloging-in-Publication Data
Names: White, Aaron, 1976– author.
Title: Recovering : from brokenness and addiction to blessedness and community / Aaron White.
Description: Grand Rapids, Michigan : Baker Academic, a division of Baker Publishing Group, 2020. | Series: Pastoring for life: theological wisdom for ministering well | Includes bibliographical references and index.
Identifiers: LCCN 2019048614 | ISBN 9781540960825 (paperback)
Subjects: LCSH: Church work with recovering addicts. | Church work with alcoholics. | Pastoral counseling. | Beatitudes—Criticism, interpretation, etc.
Classification: LCC BV4460.3 .W45 2020 | DDC 259/.429—dc23
LC record available at https://lccn.loc.gov/2019048614

ISBN 978-1-5409-6318-5 (casebound)

This book was written on the traditional territories
of the Coast Salish Peoples, including the territories
of the xʷməθkwəẏəm (Musqueam),
Skwxwú7mesh (Squamish),
Stó:lō and Səlílwətaʔ/Selilwitulh (TsleilWaututh) Nations.

These territories were never ceded to Canada
through treaty, war, or surrender.
I lift my hands to these beautiful people
and say thank you: "Huy ch q'u"

Risen from the dead are the poor in spirit . . .
Risen from the dead are they who mourn . . .
Risen from the dead are the meek . . .
Risen from the dead are they who hunger and thirst
    for righteousness . . .
Risen from the dead are the merciful . . .
Risen from the dead are the pure of heart . . .
Risen from the dead are the peacemakers . . .
Risen from the dead are they who are persecuted
    for righteousness sake . . .

Jim Forest, "Climbing the Ladder
of the Beatitudes," August 16, 2017

Contents

Series Preface

One of the great privileges of being a pastor is that people seek out your presence in some of life's most jarring transitions. They want to give thanks. Or cry out for help. They seek wisdom and think you may know where to find some. Above all, they long for God, even if they wouldn't know to put it that way. I remember phone calls that came in a rush of excitement, terror, and hope. "We had our baby!" "It looks like she is going to die." "I think I'm going to retire." "He's turning sixteen!" "We got our diagnosis." Sometimes the caller didn't know why they were calling their pastor. They just knew it was a good thing to do. They were right. I will always treasure the privilege of being in the room for some of life's most intense moments.

And, of course, we don't pastor only during intense times. No one can live at that decibel level all the time. We pastor in the ordinary, the mundane, the beautiful (or depressing!) day-by-day most of the time. Yet it is striking how often during those everyday moments our talk turns to the transitions of birth, death, illness, and the beginning and end of vocation. Pastors sometimes joke, or lament, that we are only called when people want to be "hatched, matched, or dispatched"—born or baptized, married, or eulogized. But those are moments we share with all humanity, and they are good moments in which to do gospel work. As an American, it feels perfectly natural to ask a couple how they met. But a South African friend told me he feels this is exceedingly intrusive! What I am really asking is how someone met God as they met the person to whom they have made lifelong promises. I am asking about transition and encounter—the tender places where the God of cross and resurrection meets us. And I am thinking about how to bear witness amid the transitions that are our lives. Pastors are the ones who get phone calls at these moments and have the joy, burden, or just plain old workaday job of showing up with oil for anointing, with prayers, to be a sign of the Holy Spirit's overshadowing goodness in all of our lives.

I am so proud of this series of books. The authors are remarkable, the scholarship first-rate, the prose readable—even elegant—and the claims made ambitious and then well defended. I am especially pleased because so often in the church we play small ball. We argue with one another over intramural matters while the world around us struggles, burns, ignores, or otherwise proceeds on its way. The problem is that the gospel of Jesus Christ isn't just for the renewal of the church. It's for the renewal of the cosmos—everything God bothered to create in the first place. God's gifts are not *for* God's people. They are *through* God's people, *for* everybody else. These authors write with wisdom, precision, insight, grace, and good humor. I so love the books that have resulted. May God use them to bring glory to God's name, grace to God's children, renewal to the church, and blessings to the world that God so loves and is dying to save.

Jason Byassee

Foreword

BOB EKBLAD

Aaron White's *Recovering: From Brokenness and Addiction to Blessedness and Community* is a straight-talking and passionate treatise that lays out essential components of a holistic and radically Christian approach to effective recovery from addictions of any kind. As one who has ministered among people affected by addictions for over thirty-five years, I welcome my friend Aaron's savvy, faith-filled wisdom wrought from years of living in community in the heart of North America's highest concentration of IV drug users—Vancouver's Downtown Eastside.

Aaron's writing comes out of fifteen years of compassion-filled pastoring of some of the most downtrodden and rejected people in one of North America's most beautiful and wealthy cities. As a street theologian, he has persevered and even thrived in Canada's most notorious neighborhood. Years of being in close relationship with those he serves, combined with a robust life of prayer; contemplation of Jesus; worship; and study of Scripture, theology, and anything that might bring lasting change to the most broken has qualified him to write this book.

Aaron has suffered numerous defeats as he has walked alongside the people on the streets of his neighborhood—as has anyone called to minister to people caught up in addictions. As he has pursued the gospel that truly has the power to save, his dialogue partners have broadened to include myriad fellow travelers—from active users and now recovering addicts to the academy, the church, and the nonprofit world.

With great humility Aaron has put himself under countless men and women he has encountered on the streets of the Downtown Eastside. Aaron has listened to people's stories, heard his Indigenous friends' pain born out of the dislocation of colonialism, learned from his street friends' analyses, wept with his neighbors over their losses, and rejoiced with them over their miracles and victories. This book includes both tragic stories and beautiful testimonies that inspire hope.

Aaron has made his share of mistakes and writes from a tender place that is raw and honest while at the same time hope filled. His commitment to seeing true liberation come to his neighborhood has led him to consult experts in addiction and relapse prevention, traveling the world to learn from ministries working with people struggling with addictions. He has studied key sociologists, psychologists specializing in abuse and other kinds of trauma, early church fathers who inspire Eastern Orthodoxy and Roman Catholicism, evangelical and charismatic revivalists, and biblical authors. Aaron has drunk from many wells to sustain himself on his journey, and in particular he has drawn strength from the 24-7 Prayer movement, which he has helped lead in Canada since 2001.

All this to say that Aaron White offers here potent reflections from the trenches that will help anyone working in any context with people suffering from addictions—whether you are a veteran worker serving the homeless or someone starting fresh. Yet he himself does not present this as a fix-it manual for people who are addicted but rather as an appeal to foster "the kind of environment that Jesus prescribed for his people, which happens to be exactly the kind of environment that helps us resist and heal from the brokenness of our world."

Repeatedly, Aaron argues that discipline-focused abstinence approaches alone are not enough. Rather, effective approaches will be born out of respectful listening and compassion. Deep inner healing from life's hurts together with an alternative community that welcomes people struggling with addiction are necessary. If addictions are nearly always "coping mechanisms in the form of self-medicating solutions for real pain," then we must learn to address the underlying sources of the pain that lead to addictions: the deeply wounded heart and the deeply broken community.

But we are not left without hope. Aaron presents the resurrected Jesus as the ultimate healer of the heart. He draws inspiration from Jesus's earthly life and ministry among the poor and downtrodden of Israel's margins in Galilee. Jesus's friendship with and pursuit of sinners has certainly mobilized Aaron and his community to seek lost sheep until they are found. There are, of course, many such "rescue ministries." But in this book Aaron challenges the normative idea that the goal of recovery is to help addicts—or to help anyone—become contributing and functioning members of our dysfunctional society.

Aaron's approach goes even beyond establishing transitional or relapse-prevention houses. He presents a more radical alternative, which is in alignment with the shepherd in Jesus's parable, who doesn't bring the found sheep back to the ninety-nine but brings him or her home instead: "He calls together his friends and his neighbors, saying to them, 'Rejoice with me, for I have found my sheep which was lost!'" (Luke 15:6 NASB). Aaron calls on the church to become healing homes so there are secure and nurturing destinations into which shepherds can bring their finds; he then fleshes out a vision of what he calls the "blessed" Beatitude Community—a vision drawn from Jesus's Beatitudes in the Sermon on the Mount.

Next, Aaron explores each of Jesus's Beatitudes, commenting on what it looks like here and now to join in and become an active disciple inside a blessed community of the poor in spirit. This book's most unique contribution to the literature of recovery is this well-argued assertion: the kingdom of heaven that Jesus describes is the present inheritance that must be actively offered to those whose pain has led them into further brokenness and suffering through addiction. And all of us are vulnerable and hurting to varying degrees.

Once inside, the comfort of the Beatitude Community is available to those who mourn; the earth is promised as future inheritance to the meek; fullness to those who discover that their true hunger and thirst is for righteousness; mercy for those who themselves learn to extend mercy to themselves and others; membership in a new family to those who become peacemakers; and support for those who experience ongoing trials and persecution.

This book clearly has a prophetic edge—critiquing the status quo of recovery, church, and society. At the same time, it often reads like a discipleship handbook and devotional combined—teaching, inspiring, and challenging the reader to step more fully into the divine image lived out in an alternative community that includes the most broken. May you enjoy the challenge to more fully surrender to the Jesus of the Gospels, who keeps calling you now. May you find ways to live into the abundant life as a truly alternative way that will bring real hope for healing and transformation in these dark times.

Introduction

My dad's first memory of his father is a backhand slap across the face. David White was born just before his father left to fight in the Second World War. Returning home one day at the age of five after wandering through the neighbor's cow fields, he encountered a large, uniformed man standing beside his mother in the kitchen.

"David, say hello to your father."

Before either of them spoke, my grandfather struck my dad, hard. "What were you doing outside the house!" This unpredictable anger became the norm for my dad's relationship with his father throughout childhood and into his teenage years.

By all accounts my grandfather had been a decent, God-fearing man, a member of the Salvation Army Band, and a good husband. Then he went to war, saw things that were only ever hinted at to us grandkids, and came back an angry man. A bitter, volatile man. An addicted, alcoholic man.

We grandchildren knew we had to be careful at Grandma and Grandpa's house. Grandpa was usually in the basement, his domain, and sometimes everything would be great. But sometimes we would make too much noise, or the wrong sort of noise at the wrong sort of time, and things would suddenly no longer be great. Only my little brother seemed immune from Grandpa's sudden bursts of anger: he sometimes even hid Grandpa's cigarettes without repercussion.

1

Grandpa frequented Vancouver's Downtown Eastside (DTES), the community where my family and I now live and minister. The DTES has been described as "the worst postal code in Canada" and "ten blocks of hell," but we just call it home. It features open drug dealing and use, survival prostitution, violence, and all the homelessness, food lines, and slum landlords that the rest of Vancouver wants to stay hidden. It is in part a social construction, the result of canceled national housing strategies, shuttered mental health facilities, influxes of new drugs and communicable diseases, and city efforts to contain all these issues within one location. Millions of dollars are invested each year just keeping people alive, but the lives of those stuck in poverty and addictions are not noticeably improved. The DTES is also the friendliest place I have ever lived, filled with funny, resilient, kind, generous, spiritual neighbors who know each other's names and stories. It is currently under threat from both an opioid crisis and aggressive gentrification that has squashed the neighborhood and all its challenges into smaller and smaller geography. I don't know which of these threats is worse, but I do know they are both the result of addictions.

When my grandpa came here it was to drink and get into trouble. My dad, following in his old man's footsteps, also made his way into this neighborhood and into alcoholism. My grandmother could likewise be found in the DTES, but she worked for the Salvation Army. She ministered to court workers, visited prisoners, and sometimes bailed young women out and brought them home to care for them. She was known as the Angel of the Courthouse. As with many families entrenched in addiction, their lives were a study in incoherency.

Dad and Grandpa suffered from emotional and spiritual dislocation: one from the trauma of war, the other from the trauma of a father broken by war. This is characterized within the twelve-step program as "a lack of inner experience of intimacy with oneself, with God, with life, and with the moment."[1] This dislocation is fertile ground for addiction. It ruined much of my grandfather's life and almost destroyed my dad's as well. My dad met the Lord, however, and met my mom—these two meetings coincided somewhat—and his way was mended before I was born. He was truly converted, describing the experience as becoming utterly full of the presence of

God, so full that he felt he had to flee the church building for fear of blowing off the roof. The ongoing effect of God's presence in his life was equally dramatic. I never knew my dad as an alcoholic, never knew the fear that comes with having an addicted, unpredictable parent. Still, his life, and by extension my life, was indelibly marked by his father's deep, war-born woundedness and addiction. Near the end, praise God, we witnessed Grandpa's radical transformation. His faith was renewed and his hard heart somehow softened by the grace of God, who never stopped loving and pursuing my grandpa. He ceased drinking and even rejoined the band. At his funeral, though my dad had to honestly eulogize Grandpa as a "hard and sometimes cruel man," he could also announce with joyful faith that his father was in the arms of the Savior, healed of all pain and brokenness.

I think of my grandparents and parents often as I reflect on life and ministry. I grew up attending a Salvation Army Corps (church) in Vancouver, absorbed evangelical/holiness doctrine, and promised in my Junior Soldier's Pledge to avoid "anything that may injure my body or my mind, including harmful drugs, alcohol, and tobacco." I really did stay away from harmful drugs, alcohol (for the most part), and tobacco. I can't say I was able to stay away from everything that could injure my body or mind, but my parents certainly did their level best to protect me. I was so protected that I had few meaningful interactions with anyone addicted to harmful drugs or alcohol. Our congregation was far removed from the DTES, and I don't recall much talk about addictions except that people who used drugs were to be pitied and helped, but from a distance, and usually by professionals. I learned that there were places for them, ministries and worship services for them, but that these were all separate from ours.

This was all fine and good for me, until I needed a summer job. A friend hired me to run the front desk of a homeless shelter in the DTES from 3 p.m. to 11 p.m., five nights a week. It was me, a janitor/security guard, thirty men in the shelter, a hundred or so longer-term residents, and a collection of men recently released from prison. I was eighteen years old, and I had no idea what I was doing. My life was threatened during my first shift, after which I counted the number of hours until summer was over. I may have genuinely prayed for the first time that night as well. As the summer progressed, however, I

began to make friends with the men living in the building and grew
in my understanding and appreciation of them as fellow humans.
That sounds like an odd revelation, but it's one I needed. Just like
my grandpa and my dad, these guys had hopes and dreams, could
love and be loved, and were dealing with significant pain and trauma.
Most were addicted, but they were also beloved children of God.

The following summer I worked in the same courts and prisons
where my grandma had worked, again encountering people at their
lowest moments. There are categories of "prisoner," "homeless," and
"addict" that we all make in our minds, but meeting people in the
holding cells and hearing their stories helped to break those categories
down. This has also been true as I have lived and ministered in the
DTES for the last fifteen years. My wife, my family, and I moved back
here to serve an incarnational faith community called 614 Vancouver,
named after the hopeful passage of return from exile in Isaiah 61:4:

> They shall build up the ancient ruins;
>   they shall raise up the former devastations;
> they shall repair the ruined cities,
>   the devastations of many generations.

The past fifteen years have shown us that the people who do this
building, raising, and repairing are most often the very ones whose
lives have been so wrecked by ruin and devastation. What's more,
journeying as a pastor-in-community alongside people in their addiction and recovery is the tool God has used to confront me with
my own addictions and attachments.

With permission, I will tell many of the stories of the beautiful
and broken people I have come to know as neighbors, friends, and
fellow pilgrims in the DTES and around the world. These stories
revolve around deep tragedy, and I recount them with some trepida-
tion because I do not want to romanticize or emotionally weaponize
anyone's struggle. There is this reality too: some of those whose
stories I share have died, sometimes badly, and it is possible that
some of my friends will fall back into addiction after their stories
are written down. These are snapshots of an ongoing life. This in
no way negates their truth or importance, and many of these stories

have the whiff of the miraculous about them. Even when the stories appear distinctly nondivine and nonvictorious, it is still essential to listen to the experience of those who have known the devastation of addiction firsthand. My dad's family knew this, but thanks to their recovery my childhood did not. Instead, like my grandma, I have given my life to pastoring and learning from those caught in the web of addiction. I tell my family's story because much of what we do is in response to the way we have been raised, and most people I know can trace their addiction back to the pain and brokenness of their family experience. These deep-rooted wounds are some of the factors that make recovery so difficult, yet this should not leave us hopeless.

What Does It Mean to Be Fully Human?

In this book I want to show that we have not been left alone or without resources, even in the face of trauma and societal dislocation. But this is not going to be a how-to manual on "fixing" people who are addicted. Rather, this will be about creating and fostering the kind of environment that Jesus prescribed for his people, which happens to be exactly the kind of environment that helps us resist and heal from the brokenness of our world. Here is my central assumption: Beatitude Communities, based on Jesus's revolutionary blessings in the Sermon on the Mount, are the best hope for us to learn how to become fully human. This type of community answers the deep pain, brokenness, and dislocation that lies at the heart of all addictions, chemical or otherwise. Pastors and churches can cultivate this Jesus-vision of a new way of living, one that takes seriously the individual's struggle and the brokenness of the world around us, but which also takes into account God's grace and the community of faith.

The first part of this book talks about the nature of the brokenness that leads to addictions of every kind (not just drugs and alcohol) and the alternative way that God offers. The second half looks at each Beatitude in turn, showing how they build on one another and progressively address the underlying spiritual and societal causes of addictions. The order of the Beatitudes is important: they are a ladder that we climb, like the twelve steps of recovery, with each step building on the previous in a journey from the personal moment of clarity to a holy engagement with God, community, and the world. This journey teaches us to know and practice what humans are "fitted for": we are God's beloved children, made to be united with Christ, a possibility opened to us through the incarnation, death, and resurrection of Jesus. The fruit of this union is an authentic and coherent human life that seeds justice into the world. This is the way of being *blessed*, which means freedom from fear and death, and freedom to share in the life of God. What is at stake is not just recovery from drugs, alcohol, and other attachments, but the recovery of full humanity, which is the recovery of the image of the divine in each person.

Each chapter includes recommendations for ways to practice the Beatitudes personally or as a community, whether you are in addictions recovery or have never touched drugs or alcohol. Interspersed throughout as well are "Pauses" for prayers, psalms, and thoughts drawn from Scripture, church tradition, and contemporary poets. These are reminders to breathe; it is easy to get lost and even hopeless in the discussion of addictions. My hope is that this book will be read not just for information, but as an act of prayer.

Hope

A woman in the DTES stopped me on the street to talk with some urgency after noticing the Salvation Army shield on my jacket. Long ago she had been addicted and in jail, abandoned by her shamed family. To her shock, a Salvation Army worker bailed her out, brought her home, and introduced her to Jesus and a new way of living. From that moment on, everything changed for her. She told me that she had never really had the opportunity to properly thank the woman who had so opened her life and home, and she wondered if I could pass along a message. Did I know a woman named Mona White? Yes, I said, I knew her, but my grandma had passed away some years ago. Tears welled in the woman's eyes as she said, "Well then I give my thanks to you, in her place, because once I was lost, and now I am found."

So, Grandma, I dedicate this work to you, in gratitude for the example you gave me. I dedicate it to your husband, my grandpa, in recognition of the horrors he suffered that led to his near ruination. I further dedicate it to your son, my father, and to my mother, who by the love of the Savior and with the love of family gave me an upbringing free from violence and instability. Finally, I dedicate this book to my wife, Cherie, my fierce co-laborer in the gospel; my family; my community; and all my beautiful, beloved neighbors who are carrying on this courageous journey of learning and loving in Vancouver's DTES.

Friends, there is hope.

PART 1

BROKEN
AND BLESSED

Examining our world and our hearts to find the
sources of brokenness, pain, and displacement that
lead to addiction and seeking what hope may be
found.

ONE

Broken

What causes quarrels and what causes fights among you? Is it not this, that your passions are at war within you?

James 4:1

The first step 5 confession I ever heard is seared into my heart and mind. I was leading worship during a church meeting in Victoria, BC. Our congregation met near the local Addictions Rehabilitation Centre, but that was not remotely the demographic of our worshiping community. This evening, however, a stranger had somehow discovered our meeting and made his way inside. When the time came for prayer requests, the man stood up and shakily announced, "I am an alcoholic. . . . If I don't get help, I'm going to die." Then he sat down. Nobody knew what to do. Someone uttered a simple prayer for strength and courage or something, and we moved awkwardly to the next prayer request. The man sat for a while in his pew, alone, and then eventually got up and walked out. Seeing this from the front, I was self-righteously incensed. Why had no one moved to sit with this man? Why was no one following him out the front door? What is wrong with this church? And then I realized the problem with my judgment: I had not moved to sit with him; I was not following him; there was something wrong with me. I walked off the stage and ran

out of the building to find him. He was sitting on the front step, and I
scared him badly as I burst out the front door in a blaze of missional
zeal. Once we both calmed down he told me he wanted to do a step
5. Step 5 of the twelve steps is when we "admit to God, to ourselves,
and to another human being the exact nature of our wrongs." This is
what he proceeded to do, confessing the exact and horrifying nature
of his wrongs to a passionate but overwhelmed eighteen-year-old.
We spent an hour together, him talking, me listening, on that cold,
cement step. I was shocked by his vulnerability and honesty, something I had never witnessed in a church setting. At the end he let me
pray for him, then we hugged, and he left. I went back inside and
promptly broke down crying. When my pastor asked why I was so
emotional, the best I could come up with was that this was what
God wanted for that man and for our congregation, and I was so
blessed to participate. There was a gift that God had for that man
through our prayer and through my listening, and I suspect there
could have been a lot more for him had we been better prepared to
offer it. But there was also something God wanted to give to us, to
me, in that encounter, a beautiful gift that could come only through
the man's broken, honest cry and confession. That was the question
I left with that night: Are we ready to be part of the blessing God
wants to pour out on his children through real, raw encounters with
people in pain? And will we know what to do when we receive it? I
have heard many step 5 confessions since that first one, and I have
never ceased to wonder at how God uses honesty and vulnerability
to effect healing and wholeness.

You and Me

There is a frighteningly true AA aphorism: you are only as sick as
your secrets. So let's start with some honesty and vulnerability: I am
not a stranger to addiction. I have been addicted to different thought
patterns, behaviors, relationships, and things throughout my life,
some of which will be discussed in the body of this book. I do not
say this with either pride or resignation; I just say that it is true, that
I am working on it, and that by the grace of God and the help of

my community I have experienced growing freedom and hope. You have been affected by addiction too. Even if you are a pastor (or a would-be pastor), it is not simply that you have people who are addicted to drugs and alcohol in your congregation, which you most certainly do. If you are honest, you will acknowledge that there are dark areas in your heart and mind where you have little to no control. You feel trapped and hypocritical. This interior darkness is the place where most of us have hidden our addictions. Addiction does not just refer to chemical substances, so whether you are addicted to alcohol, amphetamines, pornography, control, a relationship, procrastination, your self-image, money, success, or anything else, you are still addicted. And we all live in a society with addiction enthroned at its very core: addiction to capital, to development, to celebrity, to GDP, to nationalism, to exceptionalism, and more. This is a huge concern personally, societally, and spiritually, yet it is one that very few people are willing to acknowledge and that even fewer people know what to do about. The good news is that something can be done about this—the major something has in fact already been done about this—and we can participate in our own healing, the healing of others, and even the healing of our broken society. That is the point of this book. The more difficult news, which I refuse to downplay, is that this is really, really hard work that requires absolutely everything we have. We cannot begin to help others if we do not take this work seriously in our own lives.

Addiction is a holistic issue: it affects body, soul, and spirit as well as relationships, employment, housing, finances, leisure, and all forms of societal engagement. Any response to addiction must likewise consider the fullness of the human condition. Portugal has done this with some success in the last decade by decriminalizing drugs and investing massively in treatment, prevention, housing, education, and job training for people in recovery. In Vancouver the policy around homelessness and addiction has shifted to include Housing First, which is an attempt to help people get into safer housing, without barriers, before trying to address any deeper issues. Once housed, efforts are made to help with recovery, to acknowledge the unique needs and decisions of individuals, and to integrate people into social life. This is good, but even the best government policies cannot speak to the deep wounds and desires of our hearts. We are invested with a profound longing for fulfillment, for wholeness, for kinship, and for love—longings that can only be satisfied by something outside of ourselves. This necessarily includes human community. Frederick Buechner says, "You can survive on your own; you can grow strong on your own; you can prevail on your own; but you cannot become human on your own."[1] But even human community is not enough. We were created with an inner desire for God, a deep yearning for relationship with our Creator, a relationship that contains within it our very meaning and purpose.

Knowing and pursuing our heart's divine longing is central to finding our way—and helping others to find their way—out of addiction and into recovery. Richard Rohr asserts that "spiritual desire is the drive that God put in us from the beginning, for total satisfaction, for home, for heaven, for divine union, and it just got displaced onto the wrong object."[2] That is, addiction co-opts and redirects the energy behind our created purpose. Gerald May describes it this way: "Addiction exists wherever persons are internally compelled to give energy to things that are not their true desires. . . . Addiction is a *state* of compulsion, obsession, or preoccupation that enslaves a person's will and desire. Addiction sidetracks and eclipses the energy of our deepest, truest desire for love and goodness."[3]

This applies to all addictions, not just to drugs and alcohol. Of course, there is a significant difference in degree between an addiction to social media and an addiction to heroin. Both are enslavements, but one tends to wreck your life, or even kill you, a lot quicker. And even within those general categories there are differing intensities to our addictions, and different short- and long-term consequences. At the core of this book is the assertion that addiction affects us all, personally and societally, and all our addictions should be taken seriously. Yet our eyes must be open to the acute suffering and danger experienced by those whose pain and trauma has led them to drug and alcohol addiction. There is a cost when I fall back into my old temptations and attachments, but it is still possible that nobody will even know about it except me and God. When some of my friends fall back into their old temptations and attachments, they risk losing their sobriety, their reputation, their job, their family, their sanity, their homes, and their lives. Not only this, but there is a stigma attached to drug and alcohol use that makes these addictions all the more dangerous. One of the reasons many people die when they resume using drugs after a period of abstinence is the need to keep it a secret out of fear and shame.

This has been particularly true in our neighborhood over the last few years with the influx of a powerful opioid called fentanyl, which resembles heroin but is one hundred times stronger. British Columbia was home to 3,400 overdose deaths in the past four years—in 2017 the province averaged four fatal overdoses per day, over 1,500 for the whole year—with roughly a quarter of those deaths occurring in Vancouver.[4] As I write, there have been eleven overdose deaths in the past week. The issue is not specific to Vancouver, however. In a 2012 study, 21.6 percent of Canadians, or roughly six million people, met the criteria for a substance abuse disorder.[5] The heroin industry brings in a *reported* fifty-five billion dollars (US) annually worldwide, which is not all coming from our neighborhood. In the United States, approximately twenty million people over the age of twelve have an addiction to drugs or alcohol, with one hundred reported overdoses each day, a rate that has tripled in the last twenty years. The highest reported substance-use numbers are among those eighteen to twenty-five years old, and 90 percent started their addiction before the age of eighteen.[6] Poverty tends to increase the severity of the consequences, but addiction itself is no respecter of class, gender, age, race, or religious background—which is why I confidently say that you have people who are addicted to drugs and alcohol in your congregation. But these stats are incomplete because they only deal with one small part of worldwide addictions. When you add in other "process addictions" such as pornography, gambling, power, money, codependent relationships, overwork, food, social media, and more, you see how this affects absolutely everyone.

Pain and Dislocation

But where do these addictions come from? And why are they so powerful?

We should start by acknowledging that while we are affected by addictions, there is no such thing as a "universal addict." Each person has her or his own unique backstory and context, and each one is beautifully and wonderfully designed to reflect and carry the image of God. Let us be careful to remember the inherent dignity at the heart of every single person we meet, no matter how "lost" they appear to us.

It is still possible, however, to identify certain commonalities and shared experiences that are connected to addictive behavior. The primary common denominator for addiction is not a weak will or moral failing, but *pain*. Gabor Maté calls addiction a "stupid friend" that starts as a response to pain but then becomes an issue in and of itself.[7] Drugs, alcohol, and other substances or habits, while wreaking terrible harm on the lives of individuals, families, and communities, are not the real issue, though they often become the most pressing issue. They are, as my friends in recovery like to put it, the tip of the iceberg, but there is a lot more iceberg underneath the surface. What many people inside and outside the church fail to see is that addictions are almost always coping mechanisms in the form of self-medicating solutions for real pain.

Where does such ravaging pain come from? The most obvious answer is early childhood trauma and abuse. I know very few drug users or alcoholics who have not experienced some kind of horrific distress, and most of us understand how this could lead to sub-stance use to numb the pain. This is not, however, the only kind of pain, and many people who have suffered abuse and severe trauma do not end up in chemical addictions. We find people in drug and alcohol addictions, as well as process addictions like gambling, overeating, and self-harm, from all socioeconomic groupings. In fact, there has been an alarming growth in addictions and associated causes of death among North America's middle class since 1998.[8] This is because everyone, from every background in our society, is familiar with pain, but we are growing increasingly unfamiliar as a culture with how to handle it emotionally, psychologically, socially, and spiritually. Brené Brown, writing after the suicide of famous designer Kate Spade, said, "To know pain is human. To need is human. And, no amount of money, influence, resources, or sheer determination will change our physical, emotional, and spiritual dependence on others."[9]

But what if the deck is stacked against us when it comes to dealing with pain, depending on others, and finding healing? Bruce Alexander, whose Dislocation Theory of Addiction is of seminal importance, argues that we need to start asking *why* it is increasingly difficult in our society for vast numbers of people to avoid addictions, and not only to drugs and alcohol.[10] Historical evidence suggests that the whole range of addictions is far more common within unjust, broken, or tyrannical societies; the breakdown of cultures through war, economic disaster, colonization, or other causes has led to widespread dislocation and addiction in every age. Alternatively, when a culture or society is functioning well, when there is evidence of cooperation, balance, and a commitment to the common good, addictions are far less prevalent.[11]

Even the World Health Organization is beginning to accept that the fragmentation of society and widespread social distortion explain modern health problems better than many other individualized risk factors.[12] Alexander suggests a number of reasons our current way of living leaves people so susceptible to addiction: "Beneath the steamroller of modernity, extended families and communities are scattered; nuclear families become dysfunctional; local societies are pulverized; legitimate authority is toppled; religious certainties disappear; and cultural arts salvage fragments of destroyed cultures as trinkets for tourist shops. People and social groups that do not contribute to the advance of modernity are marginalized or exterminated."[13]

One of the greatest crimes of colonialism was the undermining of traditional kinship community among Indigenous peoples, resulting in the removal of cultural supports that help people navigate trauma. Wendell Berry views this as the foundational theme of North American history: any group or culture that formed roots in kinship and the land has been repeatedly dispossessed, driven out, subverted, or exploited by "those who were carrying out some version of the search for El Dorado. Time after time, in place after place, these conquerors have fragmented and demolished traditional communities."[14] The same is happening now as traditional cultures are being displaced at historic rates in the modern refugee crisis. Those who make it to Western countries are strongly urged to abandon the culture they know in favor of our more "enlightened" liberal democracy and capitalism. Yet modern secular culture, from a sociological and anthropological perspective, has proven to be one of the weakest in history at preparing its members to deal with grief, pain, and loss.[15] Our strict materialism and lack of kinship prevents us from assigning any ultimate meaning to suffering. It can only be understood as accidental, yet inevitable; to be avoided or minimized at all costs; and primarily the preserve of experts and professionals whose job it is to alleviate our pain while we sacrifice our agency to them. Many of those same experts in the field of addictions treatment have abandoned the notion that addictions can be overcome, promoting instead the narrative of addiction as a chronic disease that can be "managed by lifelong monitoring and treatment, but not cured."[16]

This has come about because most of us have not learned healthy ways to deal with our pain, and we don't live in a world that encourages us to face our brokenness. So we adapt by looking for whatever we can find to distract or numb us. Our brains are particularly adept at this. Once we find something that will do the trick, we latch onto it and form a deep attachment that is not just physical but social, emotional, even spiritual. These attachments usurp the place that God is meant to have in our lives as comforter, giver of meaning, disturber of our self-contained reality, and recipient of worship. Then, because the object of our attachment was not designed to fulfill that role in our lives, we need more and more until we risk losing control of our relationship with it. Sometimes the addiction serves the dislocation in society—as in the case of consumerism, overwork, or social media preoccupation—so it is encouraged and rewarded. Other times the addiction makes the dislocation we feel even worse, which causes us to rely on it ever more for comfort.[17]

In other words, our society has created the conditions for pervasive trauma and is ill-equipped or ill-disposed to help people find healing in the resulting chaos. Modernity is characterized by a deep sense of displacement and purposelessness in the outer world and a general failure of family, community, and society to provide safe and sacred space, all of which is mirrored by a lack of coherence and meaning in our inner world. There is no commonly accepted "good" for which we have been created and no "just" society that we agree on or experience. Our modern worldview does not offer any real hope against the loss of meaning or substance in our relationship with ourselves, God, others, or the world around us.[18] Tim Keller offers the following summary of John Gray's point: "In the secular worldview, all happiness and meaning must be found in this lifetime and world. To live with any hope, then, secular people must believe that we can eliminate most sources of unhappiness. But that is impossible."[19] So we search, mostly without guidance, for relief from life's pain and brokenness, but also for some form of meaning, transcendence, and joy, some access to a reality greater than ourselves. Eschewing the possibility of a personal Creator, and not being connected in community, we find replacements for God and family in all kinds of places, be it chemical substances, codependent relationships, acquisition, pornography, food, control, busyness, or any number of other stand-ins. Addiction gives us a temporary escape from our feelings and a deadening of our senses, but it is only a pale substitute for life in all its fullness because none of these surrogates ultimately satisfy. We long for something more, yet we are terrified to let go of what we know, even as we grow to hate our enslavement to it. And we are terribly lonely. All of this results in a deep brokenness that distorts and veils the image of God in humanity. Titus says, "For we ourselves were once foolish, disobedient, led astray, slaves to various passions and pleasures, passing our days in malice and envy, hated by others and hating one another" (3:3).

Narratives of Pain

Michel is Métis, a people who trace their ancestry from Indigenous and European settlers. Growing up in Quebec, Michel never felt like he belonged. At school he was made to repetitively wash his hands because his brown skin was "dirty." He was sensitive to his otherness in every situation and to the exclusion his family faced. He finally found his magic elixir in grade eight when he started drinking. Alcohol gave him courage and friends, and it dulled the feeling of being isolated and unwanted. Eventually it became the substance that brought him a sense of peace. "All I needed," he says, "was my six-pack, some cigarettes, and a TV, and everything was right." Until, of course, his drinking started causing him to lose work and friends and relationships. It no longer served him; he served it. The very belonging that he craved was sabotaged by the thing that used to give him comfort, and he needed more alcohol to mask that pain. This alcoholic feedback loop sounds like a country song: "I drink because I'm lonesome, and I'm lonesome 'cause I drink."[20]

Upon entering treatment for an eating disorder, Noelle realized the connection between pain and her addiction. She used to think it was a matter of will versus compulsion until she saw how her addiction related to being hurt as a child. She could not control her surroundings or the abuse she went through, but she could control what she did or did not eat, and so she adapted ways for dealing with pain and fear that continued into adulthood. Her addictive behavior was rewarded every time someone praised her for losing weight, which happens a lot in a dislocated, image-driven society. Eventually, however, these habits came to threaten everything she knew to be good, and she had to acknowledge both the problem and the pain.

Marty did not start using any kind of drugs until he was thirty-two, but he was addicted long before that. He was obsessed with many things growing up: hockey, martial arts, water skiing, then work and the things money bought him. His father had taught him "Who you are is what you have and where you work," so he was terribly afraid of not having enough, not being good enough, and being abandoned as a result. He finally settled on cocaine to fill that gap, until he got to the point where he was ready to kill himself.

Joyce is from the Gitxsan Nation, whose people, alongside other Indigenous nations on Turtle Island (Canada), suffered theft of land, culture, language, family, and children at the hands of government and church policies. First Nations communities have survived and persevered through unbelievable abuse and pain. Joyce describes pain as ground zero: "I started drinking because I wanted to not feel the pain—the beatings, the flashbacks, the sexual abuse—I just wanted it gone. When I finally came to the end of myself I was able to quit drinking, but the pain was still there. I still remembered what happened and would live through it all over again. My friends didn't know how to help me—they were also addicted because they had been through the same things I had, like everyone else in our village. I had to find a supportive community to help me face it. No matter what, there is no shortcut around dealing with the pain."

Attachment Is a Warm Hug

An extreme example of how addictions relate to pain can be seen with heroin. Friends reliably inform me that heroin feels like a warm hug. We all like warm hugs (in fact, we *need* them), but most of my heroin-addicted friends never received warm hugs growing up. Instead, they were neglected or suffered emotional, physical, and sexual abuse from their parents, foster families, or other adults who were meant to be trustworthy. They grew up, therefore, with a glaring lack of warm, caring hugs, which became a desperate need they did not even know they had. And then, one day, they discovered heroin, and for the first time in their lives they experienced a chemical approximation of a deep, unmet desire. Imagine how strong that emotional and physical attachment would be. It was an answer to pain before it became a problem itself.[21]

I won't spend a lot of time on the biochemical aspects of addiction, but it is important to understand at least the following: "The initial attraction of drugs involves dopamine stimulation beyond the 'highs' of more normal pleasurable activities. . . . A second, more pathological phase begins when the amount of drugs increases, but the taker is in most cases still 'normal' and functioning in society. Users believe they 'have it under control.' A third and final phase involves loss of control when drug-taking becomes the individual's main goal-directed activity. . . . Drugs essentially cheat the biological purpose of reward, with natural dopamine stimulation . . . traded for a cheap hit."[22]

This is certainly true of drug addiction, which is so hard to break because it provides such an immediate, powerful, and reliable dopamine reward. But we must understand that it is also true of *all* the attachments we form to deal with feelings we don't like. We create robust psychological and emotional *grooves* between our pain and the substance or activity that we have adopted. As soon as we begin to feel pain, we run down the groove to "safety." Eventually we use the groove not simply to deal with pain but just to feel normal, and the temporary reprieve from pain becomes a habit. The state of addiction is created, according to May, when "the energy of our desire becomes attached, nailed, to specific behaviors, objects or people."[23] The concept of *attachment* is helpful because it shows that this process is not confined to chemical dependency. Alcohol and drugs are the most obvious, visible substances of addiction, but we make a mistake when we only think of addiction in these terms. Our habits, thought processes, defense mechanisms, and worldviews are also powerfully addictive.[24] If you have a hard time accepting that you are addicted, maybe you can accept that you have habitual attachments that you run to when you are depressed, scared, bored, or in pain. Do you ever find yourself eating when you are not hungry? Mindlessly scrolling through social media? Keeping yourself busy to avoid dealing with something? That is attachment. Comedian Russell Brand, a confessed black belt in addictions, describes his behavior this way: "'I'm lonely—have sex', 'I'm sad—get drunk', 'I'm bored—eat a cake.'"[25] The opposite of addiction isn't just sobriety but *connection*. Brand continues, "In our addictive behaviours we are trying to achieve the connection . . . the bliss of a hit or a drink or of sex or of gambling or eating, all legitimate drives gone awry, all a reach across the abyss, the separation of 'self', all an attempt to redress the disconnect."[26] This will never bring the transcendent meaning or true comfort for pain that we crave, but it is an incredibly powerful motivator.

More Than Detox

Given this understanding of addiction as a response to pain and a measure of our dislocated society, we can see that it is not enough to remove access to the offending substance; if it were, then a short stay in detox would suffice. This does not suffice because while the immediate issue may be the harms caused by drugs and alcohol (or any other attachment), the deeper truth is the wounded heart and the broken community. Without addressing brokenness, trauma, and dislocation, no amount of self-discipline or programs or abstinence will ultimately help people find freedom and wholeness. In fact, removing the addictive substance means removing the one coping mechanism that has worked to keep the overwhelming pain at bay. Brand was surprised to hear a counselor tell him, "How clever of you to find drugs. Well done, you found a way to keep yourself alive."[27] We should be extremely cautious about taking away this option unless we are prepared to offer a demonstrably better alternative for dealing with pain and dislocation. We should also be cautious because quitting substances cold turkey, particularly alcohol, benzodiazepines, and barbiturates, can lead to serious medical problems, including severe depression, delirium tremens seizures, and death. I was at a large prayer event one summer where international preachers and local pastors were praying over Vancouver from the stage. One pastor, praying about addictions in the DTES, asked the Lord "to supernaturally remove all the drugs right now!" A huge cheer went up from the assembled crowd, but my heart sank. It displayed such a lack of awareness of where the true issue lies, the painful reality that so many people face, and the actual work we need to do to live differently. When I ask my friends in recovery what would happen if God answered such a prayer, they all respond with some variation of "so many people would die or just find their drugs somewhere else." Alexander agrees, warning that "without their addictions, many dislocated people would have terrifyingly little reason to live, and would risk succumbing to incapacitating anxiety, depression, or suicide."[28] If that's not a damning indictment of our society, I don't know what is.

Harm reduction is one way that people have sought to respond to this. The idea is to focus not on the substances themselves, but on the harm caused by their use.[29] This can mean anything from clean needle exchanges to prescribing illicit drugs, and many other steps in between. I know many Christians and people in recovery who distrust this concept, and others who believe it is the only reasonable and compassionate response to addictions and the overdose crisis. At its best, harm reduction is an attempt to keep people alive and healthy enough to carry on, with the hope that some can reach a point where they are able to seek more permanent treatment for their addiction.[30] Harm reduction also tries to shift the power dynamics in the addiction and treatment world so that the voices of those who are most vulnerable get heard. In truth, most "mercy work" is an attempt to reduce harm, an effort to make what is unmanageable slightly more manageable. We accept shelters and food distribution programs because we want to reduce the harmful effects of homelessness and hunger, even though these are not long-term solutions. In Vancouver, and increasingly in urban centers around the world, safe injection sites allow people to use drugs under the observation of medical staff. There is also widespread use of prescribed synthetic drug replacements such as methadone and suboxone, which can help relieve some cravings and withdrawal pain, and there is even new research being done into *ayahuasca*, a hallucinogenic substance used in South and Central American Indigenous medicines for generations.[31] I don't love these strategies or the need for them. However, I have friends who are alive because of a safe injection site, friends who got free of their addictions because their lives were preserved to fight another day.

But this cannot be our long-term hope. Safe injection sites are a coping strategy, and nobody claims they are the ultimate answer for helping people overcome pain, trauma, or dislocation. The same applies even to detox, recovery programs, and Housing First strategies. If the deep pain and unmet needs at the heart of each person are not addressed and if the broken environment and alienation that surround us are left fundamentally unchallenged and unchanged, there will be no lasting freedom. I do not dream of a society in which the best we can do is house people in shelters, feed them in soup kitchens, and medically monitor them as they service their addiction.

But the trouble goes even deeper. Much of the thinking around addiction, even in the church, is based on the idea that recovery means cleaning people up so that they can be reinserted into society as fully contributing individuals. But if the dislocation of our society is such a major factor in driving people to addictions, is it something we should be trying to fit into? The recovery programs I know best offer professional counseling, employment training, schooling, twelve-step meetings, volunteering, shared meals and rooms, peer groups, and a little bit of spirituality thrown in. There is an attempt to foster community, and if clients can join a local church so much the better. But after three to twelve months the graduate is normally transitioned to independent living with an expectation of reentrance to the job market and "normal" life. Some alumni support is available, and some graduates are employed by recovery programs, but in general people are left to sink or swim within the same broken social and economic environment that alienated them in the first place. The immediate issue of drugs or alcohol may be addressed in this scenario, but the person often remains largely unchanged, partly because there is not enough time to learn a whole new way of being. Recidivism rates are high.

Most churches, if they think about addictions and recovery at all, are on board with this programmatic approach, and some are willing to go further by offering faith-based groups like Freedom Sessions and Celebrate Recovery. Much good is done within these programs. What is generally lacking from the church, however, is an analysis of why addiction is so prevalent; an understanding of how dangerous our dislocated world is to all of us; and any thought of how our social, economic, and political life could be arranged in a healthier, holier way. I suspect this is because we are unwilling or unable to examine our own addictions to the corrupting ways of the modern world. We have learned to get along in it and even to benefit from it. This is not the gospel life to which we have been called. We must learn to become far more careful and critical of the world around us, of our attachments within it, and of how these may be at odds with an allegiance to the kingdom of heaven.

Listening and Committing

"The moment one says, 'This is what it was like for me,' a rebirth occurs. Locating our wounds leads us to the gracious place of fragility, the contact point with another human being. When we share these shards of excavation with each other, we move into the intimacy of mutual healing."[32]

When honestly considering all the above factors, the pastoral situation seems bleak. All we have to do is help people through their devastating trauma while exploring the depth of our own brokenness, in the context of a dislocated society that offers distraction instead of guidance or real answers to addiction? Where do I sign up? This feeling should not be quickly dismissed, because many in our world are dealing with exactly that level of hopelessness. Gabor Maté's groundbreaking book, *In the Realm of Hungry Ghosts*, begins with story after story of the tragedies and trauma that shaped the lives of drug users and alcoholics in Vancouver's DTES.[33] I wept repeatedly as I read it, not simply because it is so shockingly sad, but because I recognized the stories and know hundreds of others whose stories are similar. I have one friend who so despaired over the suffering in his neighborhood that he resorted to preaching that crack cocaine was too big a thing for God to overcome this side of glory. He has since relinquished his faith.

If we are not prepared to risk entering the reality of the addicted in our midst and to let it challenge our own attachments and assumptions, then the pastoral vocation is not for us. *Listen* to those who are aware of their own addictions. Try to see them, to recognize their dignity, to hear the pain and longing behind their words. You won't always get the truth—some drug users lie, and some have no idea what they are talking about, just like every other segment of the population. But we have no chance if we won't even hear each other. One of my friends told me that at her lowest point, the most meaningful thing my wife and I said to her was, "We don't know what to do, but we are committed to you." Listening and committing are two of the most important tools we have when addressing addiction, and two of the most underused. They help us to overcome our fear of "the other" and to stop treating people as commodities, projects, stereotypes, jokes, horrors, or enemies. To listen to someone is to start seeing them as a sibling. As fully human.

Every year we do a "community exegesis," which involves mapping out our neighborhood, talking to residents and business owners, asking people what their dreams and fears are for the DTES, and analyzing census and demographic information. One year we discovered there were over 150 weekly AA or NA groups meeting within easy walking distance of our office. This is the kind of information that any church should know about their community, and it mostly requires paying attention to your neighbors. Jesus paid attention:

the Samaritan woman, the demoniac, the bleeding woman, the blind man—Jesus heard their real cries, knew their real pain, and did not deflect them with false piety or take advantage of their vulnerability. Like many of our neighbors, these people were used to "being either invisible or hyper-visible, but rarely just visible."[34] They were an inconvenience, at best the recipient of charity, but certainly not welcomed into spiritual community. Jesus saw beyond their immediate circumstances into the deeper hurt and need, spoke healing into that reality, and enabled them to experience true revelation and conversion.

I had a revelation and conversion when we first moved to the DTES. My wife was out and I had put our three children to bed. From the alley below our sixth-story window I heard a strange noise. I looked out and saw a woman, her bone-thin arms flailing and her body stumbling among the dumpsters as she groaned mournfully. We later heard this type of movement described as a "drug-dance" or a "devil-dance." I could not leave the children alone in the apartment, so I began to pray for her, and as I did so I was struck by this thought: If the liberating gospel of Jesus Christ can mean nothing to this desperate woman, strung out on a bad hit in a stinking alley of the DTES, then it means nothing to me. Somehow, this must be good news to both of us. Somehow, we both must be able to receive the blessing and be part of a new way of living, a new type of community. As I was contemplating this frightening revelation, my two-year-old daughter, Ciara, joined me at the window, having been wakened by the sound of the woman's crying. "What happening?" she asked, trying to look down into the alley below. I had to decide in a moment if I wanted my little girl to be initiated so early into this painful reality. "Honey, see that woman down there? She hurts so much she took some poison to feel better. But she is wrapped up in chains now, and only Jesus can help her to be free." I was not sure how much my daughter understood, but the next question she asked is the one so many fail to ask: "What her name?" To my daughter, this woman was not just an addict, not a homeless person, not a junkie—she was named. She was someone who could be known and loved. And then she asked, "Daddy, we tell her?" My daughter, in her two-year-old understanding, knew that if we could see someone's pain and knew where healing could be found, then we had to let them know. She knew that this woman was not exempt from freedom and love. And I had to believe that she was created to bear the image of God just as I or anyone else was. This became not only a conversion moment for me but also the foundation of our ministry with those in addictions here in the DTES: know people's names; see and acknowledge their pain; offer the healing that is in the gospel; and work together to see the full restoration of the image of God in one another.

Our community has not always done this faithfully or well. We have learned that the best thing we can offer a hurting world is the willingness to submit our own pain and sin to the cleansing and healing work of the gospel. We have realized, painfully, that we are up against a whole broken and dislocated system, and that this dislocation exists every bit as much inside the church as outside it. Yet we are convinced that meeting real heartbrokenness with the real love and presence of Jesus is the true work of recovery, pastoral care, and Christian community.

What to Do?

1. *Read your neighborhood.* This involves prayer-walking the streets and asking questions of neighbors, business owners, and anyone who is invested in your part of town. Find out people's hopes and fears for the neighborhood. Ask what they think about or know about addictions in the neighborhood and do some demographic research to get some real stats. See if you can identify some clear evidence of a dislocated society.[35]

2. *Look for the person of peace.* Luke 10:1–16 contains Jesus's instructions to his disciples on mission. They were to look for a person of peace, someone who would welcome them and offer hospitality. We can do that in our own neighborhoods. Be attentive to who offers you hospitality and seek to accept it with humility. This can be a good way to learn things about your community that you did not know before and can lead to friendships that bring peace to a larger, more diverse group of people.

PAUSE

Take a moment to meditate on this excerpt from a poem by the late Bud Osborn, a legendary warrior-poet in Vancouver's DTES.

yesterday I watched a woman
on the 100 block of east Hastings[36]
stand in the alley
between the Roosevelt hotel
and the Carnegie community centre
her thick black hair
was wild
her clothes were dirty and disheveled
her feet and legs were bare
and covered with bruises
and scabs and sores and running wounds
her feet were swollen
she could hardly move
and I could feel the pain
vibrating the air from each step she took
she moved like a jungle sloth
almost imperceptibly
in slow motion
and even the action
of lifting one foot
quaked with suffering
she winced
her entire body reacted with hurt
and then she placed her foot
on the filthy cobblestones of the alley
and she shuddered and tottered
staggered by pain
and this woman
is the real enemy of society
what this culture
endeavours to conceal
pain

the pain this society produces
like it produces automobiles or television shows
the pain
our pain
so vast so huge so immense
it is as though this society was constructed
to produce suffering
lonely suffering
depressed suffering
soul suffering
traumatic suffering
mental suffering
grief-stricken suffering
seduced suffering
buried suffering
addicted suffering
heart suffering
expendable suffering
insomniac suffering
angry manic fearful anxious suffering
and there is a veritable mega-industry
employed to deal with
just one day's pain in Vancouver
to conceal the pain
to confine it
to hide it
to tranquilize it
to privatize it
in psychologists' and psychiatrists' offices
in counselling centres and group therapies
on the crisis phone lines
in the 12-step groups
in the bars and taverns and pubs
in the pharmacies and drug stores
where entire shelves and aisles are devoted
to pain relief
and pain killers

pain screams that this is not a culture of life
but of death
not a culture of health but of misery
and pain exposed and expressed
subverts the lies of the media that say:
'look at us
we're happy and comfortable and pain-free
what's wrong with you?
you better do something about it'
pain cuts through the divisions
pain cuts across class race age gender
pain is where we can
identify with each other
a woman I know who lives in point grey[37]
said she has never lived in the downtown eastside
or any place like it
but when she hears people from there
speak about the pain they feel
she knows those same feelings in herself
but this wretched woman
in the alley of the 100 block of east Hastings
explodes the lies
her pain is naked
her pain is exposed
her pain is dangerous
her pain reveals the cover-up
her pain
her pain
is our pain[38]

TWO

Blessed

Seeing the crowds, he went up on the mountain, and when he sat down, his disciples came to him.

And he opened his mouth and taught them, saying: "Blessed . . ."

Matthew 5:1–3

What we see in the description of addiction and attachment in the previous chapter is a way of living and dealing with pain that works for a while but ultimately keeps us from experiencing true liberation and purpose. Worse, it is sustained and even promoted by the dislocated social, economic, political, and religious systems we have in place. We are encouraged to be displaced and distracted at every turn; to be endlessly busy, entertained, and consuming; to numb our pain; and to seek purpose in temporary pursuits. There is no agreed-on cure for addiction because it is so wrapped up in this fundamentally broken and harmful world system. For many people drugs or other attachments are the most obvious and available solutions to the pain that seems to have no other answer. Managing and mitigating people's pain within this system is therefore noble and necessary work, but the church is called to even more than this. As Laurel Dykstra points out, "A system based on domination cannot be fixed, but we can offer alternatives. Winning is not the overthrow of empire; it is any action that suggests the empire is not the only way."[1] Our deeper vocation, therefore, is to offer an alternative way of being that both heals troubled hearts and challenges the universal claims of the broken kingdom.

I call this alternative *Beatitude Community* after Jesus's list of blessings in the Sermon on the Mount (Matt. 5:1–12). Recovery communities understand that a wholesale renewal of heart, mind, lifestyle, and relationships is necessary for those addicted to drugs and alcohol. The Beatitudes show that a complete reorientation of life is no less necessary for those who have been conformed to the dislocation of the world. We have been thinking, believing, and participating in ways that lead to death; our lives don't just need a good cleaning, they need a resurrection. I have taken many people in recovery through the Beatitudes because they point the way toward this resurrected life, offering a potent cocktail of challenge and comfort to wounded and enslaved hearts. They cause us to unflinchingly face the pain and struggle of existence but also highlight beauty and hope where the world sees only ugliness and despair. Addictions result from pain and dislocation in the broken kingdom; Jesus's Beatitudes offer healing and relocation in the kingdom of heaven.

Makarios and *Theosis*

Jesus uses the word *blessed* differently than we do. The Psalms and Proverbs often distinguish the blessed from the wicked and outline the many benefits that will come to the blessed in this life, such as health, prosperity, good harvests, faithful spouses, and obedient children. Many Christians today still believe that material prosperity must inevitably accompany faithfulness. But look at the list of the blessed in the Beatitudes (expanded translation mine):

> Blessed are the poor in spirit, who know their own desperation and their need.
>
> Blessed are those who mourn, who are wrapped in sorrow, either from deep loss or from the recognition of sin and brokenness.
>
> Blessed are the meek, who live vulnerably but without compromise in the face of power and aggression.

Blessed are those who hunger and thirst for righteousness, who know that without God the world will die of spiritual hunger and dehydration.

Blessed are the merciful, who forgo wrath and embrace compassion in a world that rewards and romanticizes vengeance.

Blessed are the pure in heart, who seek holiness in a profoundly impure world.

Blessed are the peacemakers, who challenge outrageous violence and hatred with the hope of *shalom*.

Blessed are the persecuted, insulted, slandered, and falsely accused, who join Jesus in picking up their cross.

It doesn't sound very blessed. Yet this is the starting point of Jesus's sermon, this flipping of the world's expectation on its head. The blessed life, according to Jesus, includes pain, mourning, persecution, frustration, temptation, defeat, and struggle; and he incarnates this truth as fully as possible in his own life and death. Interestingly, though Jesus's description of the blessed life sounds counterintuitive to us, it resonates in a strange way with the lives of many people struggling with addictions, who are well acquainted with vulnerability, insult, sorrow, desperation, hunger, and thirst. Jesus's blessings encompass all of this, the whole of the human experience, and reveal that our pain and longing do not *have* to lead us to addiction. We were made for so much more than addiction, infinitely more than addiction. Our genuine desires can and should lead us toward the proper satisfaction of those desires. Our deepest longings for comfort, satisfaction, mercy, identity, security, a vision of God, and union with Christ are available to us, even promised to us. To get there, though, we must walk faithfully through the firm realities of life, and we cannot follow the path that our dislocated world has mapped out for us. We need to follow a different way. The blessed way.

If this is true, then understanding and embodying Jesus's blessings is essential to pastoring anyone, especially those who are addicted, because we are all entangled in the chains of the broken kingdom. Receiving Jesus's blessing seems to be the only way out of this situation. So what does Jesus mean by *blessed*? The word in Matthew's Gospel, according to Jim Forest, derives from the Greek term *makarios*. This refers to the life of the gods, which is beyond suffering, anxiety, and even death.[2] *Makarios* also describes humans who were dead and in paradise and the wealthy elite whose lives were barely imaginable to the common person. Gods, the glorious dead, and the 1 percent—all occupying space that is inaccessible to most people, all living on the favored side of an uncrossable gulf. I know many people today who still view the world in these terms. There is a common vocabulary in our culture that speaks of people being "blessed" with wealth or with abnormally good athletic, intellectual, or aesthetic gifts. Drug users and alcoholics often see themselves on one side of a chasm and the "normies" on the other side. They believe they can never have access to that fortunate life. One friend told me that every time he walks into a room he looks around to determine how everyone is better than him and why they would not want to be his friend. He believes there is a good life out there, but not for him. Another friend yells out "Lucky b——!" whenever he hears that someone has died, because he longs to be beyond pain and anguish. He won't kill himself, but he frequently prays for death.

Jesus's blessing cannot mean a life that is inaccessible or available only to a few. It is not the wealthy, the elite, the gods, the "normies," or even the typically religious who show up in the Beatitudes. Blessing is announced over the poor in spirit, the meek, the persecuted, the peacemakers, those who mourn. That which seemed wholly inaccessible is now available by the word of Jesus, specifically to those who are in the most desperate situations.

What is this accessible blessing, and how does one get it? It is freedom from the slavery to fear, pain, and death, the very thing that leads us into our attachments and addictions (2 Tim. 1:7). To grasp the scope of this promise it is helpful to look at other ways to render the word *blessed*. Jim Forest uses the phrase "risen from the dead" as a substitute for "blessed."[3] If you have already died to your old life and joined Christ in his resurrected life, there is nothing more to fear (Gal. 2:20). Ron Dart catches something of this by replacing the word *blessed* with the phrase "the Divine Life."[4] This emphasizes that humans are created to participate in the life of God, a life wherein our choices need no longer be driven by fear, pain, and death. This is the *makarios* life, which in the Beatitudes is planted firmly upon the lowly and the insignificant, in all their meekness, persecution, mourning, and poverty of spirit.

The New Testament maps out the implications of this blessed participation in the life of God in a way that makes theologians nervous and the average pastor suspicious of heresy. For instance, 2 Peter 1:4 makes the staggering claim that believers "may become partakers of the divine nature, having escaped from the corruption that is in the world because of sinful desire." Gregory of Nazianzus coined the term *theosis* to try to come to grips with the enormity of this promise. *Theosis* describes salvation as God moving into the life of humanity, which allows humanity to move into the life of God. This dual movement results in nothing less than the transformation of believers into God's likeness.[5] Athanasius also explored this radical idea, affirming that God's great gift was sharing his own image with humanity through Christ's incarnation.[6] Symeon the New Theologian wrote movingly of the beauty of *theosis* in the tenth century: "So uniting with your body, I share in your nature, and I truly take as mine what is yours, uniting with your divinity."[7] John Wesley believed that through the Spirit we can know such renewal of our hearts and minds in God's image that we can walk in the full likeness of the One who created us.[8] John Milbank explains it this way: "God in the Incarnation gave his divinity to our humanity, so divinizing it that we in turn can truly give our humanity back to God."[9]

Theosis fleshes out the biblical notion that *in Christ* humanity is made into something new (2 Cor. 5:17). The promise of salvation is not that we get marginally improved while we wait to die and go to heaven. Rather, in Christ we engage in the life of God from within, and that changes the way we live now. We take off the old self—our former corrupt way of living that was enslaved to deceitful desires—and put on a new self that is made in God's holy likeness (Eph. 4:22–24). This new self is not brought about by our own white-knuckling efforts but by Christ's invitation to share his life within the Trinity. This is what we were made for, and there simply is no higher gift or calling.

Union with Christ makes sense of the Beatitudes. Who embodies the Beatitudes more than Jesus? Who is poorer of spirit, more mournful, meeker, hungering and thirsting more for righteousness, more merciful, purer of heart, more of a peacemaker, and more persecuted for the sake of righteousness? Christ does not just bless the broken; he *is* the broken. And Christ is also the exemplar of the "blessed": the inheritor of heaven and earth, the son of God, the comforted, the fulfilled. He is the perfect picture of what it means to be fully human in our brokenness and blessedness. *Makarios* and *theosis* therefore describe how we humans are invited to share in the blessed cruciform life, death, and resurrection of Jesus. It is God's desire to be in loving fellowship and unity with his restored children, which matches our desperate human need to be loved and made free and whole in communion with our Creator.

PAUSE

"Jesus takes our humanity into heaven so that heaven can inhabit our humanity. The kingdom life of the world to come is now within us as is Jesus himself . . . not as a wonderful thought, not symbolically, not even by imitation, but truly."[10]

Participation and *Epektasis*

What does this have to do with addictions and recovery? We need a bigger vision for humanity if we want to know freedom and to communicate freedom to others. Just stopping drugs, alcohol, pornography, codependency, or whatever our attachments are is not enough. Recovering our humanity requires us to imagine and experience an entirely different way of living wherein our attachments stop making *sense*—in fact, they get in the way—because we have found something infinitely better. Jesus's Sermon on the Mount does just this, giving a vision for how humans were created to live in his image that defies the assumptions of the broken world. His way is not an obligation or a burden but rather heaven's answer to the pain, dislocation, and sin that lead to addiction. Athanasius claimed that partaking in the life of our Maker is the only truly happy life.[11] One gets the sense in some Christian circles that being one with Christ is an entirely theoretical thing, to be sung and prayed about but only actually realized after death. But listen to Kenneth Tanner's testimony of the practical effects he has known through union with Christ:

> Our union with Jesus, as we draw by grace on the new humanity he has taken with him into heaven—that kingdom that also now resides in us by his presence in us—grants us freedom from the wounds and sins of the past and the worries and fears of the future, helps us to resist the temptation to escape the present in destructive ways, disciplines us to live in the moment, that we might be aware of and available to the work of the Spirit, ready to cooperate with him in the renewal of all things.[12]

That sounds like an extraordinarily powerful alternative to the life of dislocation, attachment, and addiction! Surely this is the way that we should *want* to live. But can we? Or is this a life that God bestows only on certain blessed people, like saints in paintings and monks perched on poles in the wilderness? Our current lives, trapped in drugs and alcohol or embroiled in some other addictive snare, seem impossibly far from this ideal. Union with God sounds wonderful, but we have not experienced it.

The church fathers and mothers understood this tension and used another word to help fill out the picture of blessing: *epektasis*. This is Gregory of Nyssa and his elder sister Macrina's doctrine of spiritual progress, and it deals with the eternal, unceasing development of our happiness.[13] This means that though we are blessed here and now, there is always room for our souls to expand and to experience greater blessing and happiness as we continue to participate with God. God has reached out to us in love, and our souls may respond by stretching forward continuously toward him. We will always want more of God, and it is this that keeps us moving toward our created purpose. All we know in this life is imperfection, yet this does not stop us from pressing on every day toward the goal of union with God, which is the life for which Christ took hold of us (Phil. 3:12–14).

Epektasis is not about becoming sober, more ethical, or a more productive, tax-paying citizen. It is about continually seeking and finding more of Christ and being transformed by his Spirit into greater Christlikeness: "And we all, with unveiled face, beholding the glory of the Lord, are being transformed into the same image from one degree of glory to another" (2 Cor. 3:18). In the Beatitudes we are given a path that leads us away from brokenness and toward ultimate meaning and fulfillment, which is not some unattainable human version of perfection but rather intimacy with our Creator.

Christ makes these blessings possible, but we are still expected to participate. The New Testament letters are filled with exhortations to take vigorous action in response to God's love. Paul encourages believers in Colossae to put worldly things to death (Col. 2:5–17). He tells the Philippians to participate with God as they "work out [their] own salvation with fear and trembling" (Phil. 2:12). To the Corinthian church Paul employs the metaphor of an athlete exercising self-discipline (1 Cor. 9:25–27). In the second letter to Timothy believers are compared to soldiers, athletes, and farmers, three professions not known for passivity or sloth (2 Tim. 2:1–6). Peter describes an ascending ladder of faith, virtue, knowledge, self-control, steadfastness, godliness, affection, and love for believers to practice (2 Pet. 1:5–9). Hard work is on the agenda here, which makes sense: joining Christ in the overcoming of the world is not a weekend hobby. People in recovery will understand this as well, as recovery requires our full effort and attention.

I have a friend who complained for years that God had not relieved him of his craving for crack cocaine. I asked him how he expected God to answer his prayer when he was actively resisting every avenue of help God offered him. He wanted the blessing, but on his own terms. I told him the clichéd story of the man sitting on the roof of his house, asking God to save him from the rising floodwaters but waving off the boats and helicopters that came to rescue him. My friend smiled his cheeky smile, and said, "Yeah, that sounds about right!" God has dropped us a lifeline out of our brokenness, addiction, sin, and death—something we could never do ourselves—but we still must grab hold and keep climbing every day, with every ounce of strength we have. We cannot receive the blessings of God if we are busy striving after the concerns of the world, pursuing vengeance, seeking material gain, or avoiding suffering at all costs.

Sadly, we don't really know how to live any other way or seem able to imitate Jesus under our own steam. Thankfully, God didn't just point us toward the way out; he joins us in the climb. When Jesus promises his followers that they will be filled with the presence of the Holy Spirit, he isn't just offering warm feelings during worship songs. The Holy Spirit is the indwelling presence of God and the motive power for our participation in the fully human life. I remember my two-year-old son standing under a basketball hoop, a giant (to him) basketball at his feet, looking up at the net and stretching his arms up as far as he could reach. There was nothing in the world he wanted more than to get that ball into that basket, and nothing that was more impossible for him to accomplish. His desire was utterly out of his reach. Until, that is, his father saw his desire and was moved by love to put the ball into his little hands and lift him up to the basket. We likewise cannot reach the goal of wholeness and healing—for ourselves or for anyone else—on our own without God, but when we put ourselves in the position to receive the Spirit's blessing and help, it will come. Simone Weil affirms that "we cannot take a single step toward heaven. It is not in our power to travel in a vertical direction. If however we look heavenward for a long time, God comes and takes us up."[14] Bob Ekblad, who ministers with drug users and gangsters in Skagit County prisons, says that Jesus has faith in our capacity to be changed because he knows we were made in God's image. Accepting Jesus's faith in us, weak as we are, gives us power and confidence to be transformed. This is such good news, especially for those who have learned to see themselves only as worthless.[15] I have witnessed the beautiful transformations that happen when people grasp God's desire to partner with them in the restoration of their lives. God alone can bring about our recovery and salvation, but he offers to us the dignity of taking responsibility for our part in the journey.[16]

PAUSE

"To find God is to seek him unceasingly. Here, indeed, to seek is not one thing and to find another. The reward of the search is to go on searching. The soul's desire is fulfilled by the very fact of its remaining unsatisfied, for really to see God is never to have had one's fill of desiring him."[17]

OK, But Who Lives Like This?

Strangely, it is notoriously difficult to find a Christian community that is even *trying* to use the Beatitudes as a model for living. The ethical content of the entire Sermon on the Mount is often dismissed as good but not required, or even truly possible. It is seen to represent either a beautiful but impractical ideal or an inaccessible vision of perfection that shows us the true depth of our sin and lawlessness. I understand and agree with the emphasis on God's grace as our sole hope and with the resistance to the stringent moralism that denies the human struggle and breaks people on the wheel of self-righteous piety. I have great sympathy for the frustration we all feel—and especially that my friends in drug and alcohol addiction feel—around our repeated experiences of falling. I know the reality of disappointment and relapse all too well.

Nevertheless, I contend that failing to receive the Sermon on the Mount as practical, urgent instruction for individuals and communities seriously misses and even misrepresents the life-giving teaching of Christ. We dare neither to make light of Jesus's command to deny ourselves, pick up our cross, and follow him, nor to ignore the Spirit's power to enable us to live this way, faltering and long though our journey may be. This approach threatens to leave us with "religious" lives of miserable or apathetic compromise with the world and teaches others that this is the best they can hope for in their struggle this side of glory. Suffering and weakness are real and should never be downplayed, and we must pay attention to the twelve-step warnings that none of us is perfect or immune from disaster. But . . . is there no present power in the salvation of Jesus? Is there no hope for a different kind of life in this world? And is there not a responsibility to give ourselves entirely to the possibility of this hope, both as an act of obedience and as a witness to a suffering world? Dallas Willard says, "It may take our breath away to say it, but the blessedness is possible to all now, *regardless* of what the situation may be. That is the hope of Jesus's gospel—which is not the least excuse for failing to change situations that should be changed."[18]

I hope to show how the Beatitudes neither simply help us acclimatize to a broken, dislocated world, nor have us sitting tight in a holy holding pattern until we get to heaven. Their goal is to draw us up into the life of Christ, which requires an active correction and relinquishing of our ignorance, slavery, and sin. The Beatitudes are not a pick-and-mix spirituality wherein each blessing can be sampled in isolation. They are a step-by-step road map for living in union with Jesus and recovering the image of God in us.[19] This way will not make our lives easier, but it will help us to live well, to live healthy, and to live holy. This is God's answer to the fear and pain of the human condition.

Which leaves us with the awkward question: If the church does not believe that the Beatitudes are the prescription for a healthy and holy life, do we have anything to offer that the rest of the world cannot give? We claim in our songs that we have been set free from slavery to fear and death, but I have met few people who genuinely claim this freedom. After all, they say, we are only human. Who could live as Jesus proposes? We seem to be back into the realm of the inaccessible *makarios*, with holiness and health an ideal that doesn't match our daily reality.

My response is that many of the men and women I know in recovery *are* trying to live like this. They are doing the hard work of soul discovery and mind renewal in ways that make them seem more like monks than drunks. As a result, they have grasped hold of spiritual blessings that I have rarely seen in the church. But they need help. They need more than just a spiritual awakening. They need communities that can receive and support them and believe with them in the possibility of transformation. They need communities that know a Higher Power by name and have experienced his liberation. They need communities that are willing to admit they *need* help. In other words, they need the church to be the church, the place of genuine Jesus-blessing. And the church needs the blessing brought by these spiritual pilgrims-in-recovery as well. There is nothing more challenging and life-giving than an infusion of people who have walked a hard road, confessed to weaknesses and faults, and found deliverance and hope. This kind of vulnerability and honesty can provoke godly sorrow and repentance among the rest of us comfortable addicts. It can make us take seriously the life-altering promises of our faith and the attachments that are keeping us from accessing those blessings.

PAUSE

"We have all known the long loneliness and we have learned that the only solution is love and that love comes with community."[20]

Kinship

We need each other because the Beatitudes are not simply an individual affair. There is a reason people generally do not have success in recovery alone but form recovery communities. There is a reason dislocation and a lack of kinship and family are so disastrous in our society. Secular experiments in treating addiction through peer-based community have proven extremely successful in places like San Patrignano, Italy. San Patrignano is not a Christian endeavor, but it describes itself as "a community for life that welcomes those suffering from drug addiction and marginalization and helps them to once again find their way thanks to a rehabilitation programme that is above all, a programme based on love. It is free, because love is a gift."[21] The minimum stay in the program is three years, during which time a new pattern of life is built through daily interactions with peers and supervisors, volunteer activities, education, and loving communal coexistence. Thousands of people ensnared in their addictions have discovered freedom through this simple expression of community. How much more should the church be offering kinship community to the world if we believe we were made for Beatitude Community with one another and with God? This is why Gregory Boyle, founder of Homeboy Industries, the world's largest gang intervention, rehab, and re-entry program, says, "We don't prepare for the real world—we challenge it. For the opposite of the 'real world' is not the 'unreal world' but the kinship of God."[22]

If addiction is a way for people to deal with pain and to adapt to or replace that which is missing in their lives, then the creation of welcoming, located communities should help reduce the need for these "addictive compensations."[23] Beatitude Community is a place where pain is permitted, experienced, lamented, and overcome together;

where the dislocation of our world is rejected and exchanged for genuine shalom and kinship; and where we can mature together into the body of Christ. What if this is how we grow to learn and experience God's love, a perfect love that drives out all fear? And what if we could challenge the fear and control of the broken world with this life-giving message? Our primary calling is not sobriety; it is to be loved and companioned by God, to follow Christ, and to know and share the liberation that his love brings. It is this beatific vision of God's love for us, embodied in Christ, empowered by the Spirit, and experienced in community, that enables us to be free.

I know of many Beatitude Communities nestled in some of the most desperate neighborhoods of our dislocated world. It makes sense to find these alternative communities in places like Vancouver's DTES; in the gang- and drug-ridden Cape-Colored community of Manenberg, South Africa; with the Saint Stephen's Society in Hong Kong; in depression-era New York alongside Dorothy Day; in the impoverished neighborhoods of Cambodia; or in the famine-racked Caesarea of Saint Basil's day. These are all obvious places for Christians to help people process their pain in the light of God's promises because the dislocation is so evident. But these are not the only places that need Beatitude Communities. My friend Joe Steinke talks about growing up in suburban America with parents who made a home and family for broken people coming out of crisis and confusion. Their household was a place of nurture, healing, and sanctuary for everyone, no matter the season or socioeconomic status. Most of the recipients of this hospitality were not poor but had lost their way in the spiritual apathy of middle-class America. They were refugees of a displaced and broken land, only this land had two-car garages in cul-de-sacs, and the chasing terrors wore names like materialism, nationalism, the myth of progress, corporate Christianity, and the death of dreams. All of this was a perfect breeding ground for depression, hopelessness, and addiction. The Steinke home, therefore, became a space of familial therapy. Guests would join in the family's rule of life, the ordered rhythm and discipleship of meals, communion, pilgrimage, creativity, learning, and giving. The Steinkes believed that spiritual and emotional adoption was the only genuine delivery system of love for these orphans. This could not be done in fifty-minute sessions or in Sunday encounters but took years of time, trial, and tears. They were willing to give that time because they trusted that Christ had already forged the basis of this spiritual community in his incarnation.

The Steinke household demonstrates the level of commitment that is required to help people find freedom from addictions and attachments. We are social creatures, and when we are isolated we get in trouble, which is why "God settles the solitary in a home" (Ps. 68:6). Creating "home" takes a huge personal and relational investment that engages people physically, socially, emotionally, psychologically, practically, politically, and spiritually. Rob and Amy Reardon, pastors who oversee the Charis Recovery House in Seattle, affirm that while professional addictions counseling is important, faith communities can and should offer something very different: relationship, connection, belonging, and invitation to home and family.[24] This commitment cannot come from one person but needs to involve whole communities working together to set a new culture. A common thread of Beatitude Communities is that they cultivate environments in which people may experience mutual transformation. Saint Stephen's Society likens this to recreating family, understanding that it is often in our first experience of family that we experience the world's brokenness.[25] Most people describe authentic Beatitude Communities as "home."

Just like our biological families, however, every community I reference will have made many terrible mistakes along the way. All will have operated to some degree out of their own fears, strivings, attachments, and addictions, and will have hurt people profoundly. The difficulty of extricating ourselves from the gravity of our broken world's systems and thought patterns must not be underestimated, and we are never finished examining our own motives and commitments. I know this is true of our community here in Vancouver, and of myself more than anyone.

Lord, have mercy.

But there has also been joy and victory. This is important because wading through our attachments and struggling toward a genuine experience of Beatitude Community is the hardest thing any of us have ever tried. We are far from perfect, but we are at least still willing to ask the question that lies at the heart of this book: *What kind of people and community has God called us to be so that, united with him, we can help one another journey from broken to blessed?*

Jesus at the Party

Eleven years after we moved to the DTES we celebrated our daughter's thirteenth birthday with a Hollywood-themed party. We set up a red carpet on the sidewalk outside our house, flanked by the paparazzi (community members with cameras). Ciara and her friends dressed up in their fanciest clothes and sashayed down the block, posing for the cameras and signing autographs. Stephanie, one of our neighbors, saw the fun and came over to investigate. When she discovered it was Ciara's birthday she got very excited and asked if she could bring over a gift. We said of course and invited her in for cake and ice cream. "No," she said sadly, "I have to work. I need to get my drugs tonight." Stephanie has not hidden from us the fact that she sells sex to support her habit. She knows she is welcome in our home, but we wondered if she might feel especially out of place at a child's birthday party. She left to get the present, and we took the party upstairs. A few minutes later Stephanie knocked on the door. She had made arrangements, she said, and could maybe have a little cake? In she came. The party was in full swing, and as I looked around the room I could see teenage girls laughing their heads off; toddlers desperately trying to get into the ice cream; parents and grandparents beaming along the walls; community friends from every conceivable walk of life having fun; and this lovely woman sitting in the middle of it all, voraciously enjoying cake, grinning ear to ear, and swaying to the music. She was welcome at the party, eating the good food, having gifts of her own to offer. When she proudly gave Ciara her present, it was a moment of deep dignity and joy, the extension of family and kinship between two women at disparate ends of a dislocated society. Nothing was ultimately solved in that exchange. But I believe that for those who witnessed and partook of this small act of hope, this resistance to the broken kingdom, another step in a long journey toward Beatitude Community was taken. I believe we caught a foretaste in that moment of what it looks like to be blessed. I believe Jesus was at the party.

What to Do?

1. *Find out if there are any open AA or NA meetings in your neighborhood you can attend.* Go to listen and to see what you can learn about vulnerability and openness in the face of pain.

2. *Pray, and keep on praying.* Gregory of Nyssa taught that prayer unites us with God, which also means it separates us from the enemy.[26] Pray that God will reveal your own addictions and attachments. Pray for those you know who are sick and hurting and need God's help to find freedom. And pray for our broken, dislocated world.

3. *If you have friends and congregants who are going through recovery programs, ask how you can best support them in their program.* You don't have to become an expert in addictions or recovery methods, but you should become committed to listening and loving.

PART 2

THE BEATITUDE COMMUNITY

Looking to Jesus's Beatitudes as our hope for Christ-like and healing community.

THREE

Surrendered Community

The Poor in Spirit

Blessed are the poor in spirit, for theirs is the kingdom of heaven.

Matthew 5:3

Selling what you own, leaving your family and friends, and following Jesus is not a once-in-a-lifetime event. You must do it many times and in many different ways. And it certainly does not become easier.

Henri Nouwen, *The Road to Daybreak: A Spiritual Journey*

The first step of humility is to cherish at all times the sense of awe with which we should turn to God.

St. Benedict, *St. Benedict's Rule: A New Translation for Today*

Grace

"I'm here. This is all I can do. I made it. Please help me."

These were the words of my friend Grace, standing in our hallway, drenched with rain, exhausted, and at the end of every resource. We had arranged for her to arrive three hours earlier to stay with us as she tried to sort her life out and get into detox. When she didn't show, we suspected we would not be seeing her at all. This was not the first time we had been stood up, and it would not be the last. As it got later into the evening we lost more and more hope and got ready for bed. But then the buzzer rang. She had been wandering the rain-washed streets and alleys, trying to decide whether to give in to her cravings or to give in to hope. Finally, she bumped into a street evangelist who handed her a soggy pamphlet bearing the title "Jesus or Drugs: Your Choice." I do not generally like these judgmental-style pamphlets or the approach of the missionaries who distribute them. But I thank God for this one. She read the bold print and made the choice. It took everything she had, quite literally. She had to walk away from what she knew, let her old self die, and give herself up to whatever God might have in store for her. The image of her weeping in our hallway will always be my default for what it means to be "poor in spirit." And, therefore, what it means to be blessed.

She stayed on our couch for the next thirty days and had someone from our community next to her every single minute of that time, comforting her, praying with her, eating with her, sleeping on another couch beside her, standing outside in the rain with her during smoke breaks, going to meetings with her, and so on. We tongue-in-cheek called this our "couch program," something we had begun offering to our friends out of necessity. It started one evening after we had finished an annual mission week with a large group of teenagers, an event that never failed to exhaust our community. As we were cleaning up, a friend of mine came in. He did not look good. "Hey Aaron," he said, "I know it's not a good time but . . . I really, really need help. I have no place to go, and I'm drinking a lot . . ." He couldn't finish. He was a proud man, but his body posture spelled defeat and despair, his head hung low in shame. This was someone whose company I genuinely enjoy, one of the funniest, most well-read, most compassionate people I know. And he was really hurting, really scared, and had nowhere else to turn. We called the detox phone number, but there were no available spaces for at least a week. We have learned that people often have a window of clarity when they are ready to make a change, but if that moment is frustrated, the opportunity can slip away. So I talked it over with my wife and with people in our church community and then asked my friend if he would like to stay on our couch until a spot opened in a recovery program. Community members would stay with him the entire time to make sure he was OK. He agreed, and thus began a season where nearly every month we had a different friend staying on our couch, praying and being prayed for, joining in our family and community rhythm, experiencing transformation together.

The couch program was arduous, but it taught us something very important: as difficult as it was for our community to accompany someone around the clock, it was far more difficult for the person on the couch. Coming into our home, entering a detox or treatment center, confessing that you need help, or making any attempt to let go of your addiction requires a yielding, a surrendering of pride, a release of the illusion that you have it all under control. Poverty of spirit redresses the prideful belief that we can "out-God" God. We want to live without ultimate accountability, but as we learn in the Psalms, "The fool says in his heart, 'There is no God'" (Ps. 14:1). That verse is not simply a weapon to use against truculent atheists; it is a warning to religious folk who want to presume upon the riches of God's kindness, forbearance, and patience, forgetting that God's kindness is meant to lead us to repentance (Rom. 2:4). Poverty of spirit means repenting, laying down our arms and our pride, confessing our desperation to the Creator, and then learning the ongoing character of surrender and humility. Abba Isaac the Syrian said that we are blessed when we know our own weakness because this knowledge becomes the foundation of all goodness in us.[1]

It is no coincidence then that the first three steps in AA and NA revolve around powerlessness and surrendering one's will to a Higher Power:

1. We admitted we were powerless over alcohol/drugs—that our lives had become unmanageable.
2. We came to believe that a Power greater than ourselves could restore us to sanity.
3. We made a decision to turn our will and our lives over to the care of God as we understood him.[2]

Those who have been through recovery know full well that there can be no start without this admission, belief, and decision. If someone is not ready to admit powerlessness over their addiction, they are not yet ready to make a change. As they say in Alcoholics Anonymous, "Half-measures availed us nothing. We stood at the turning point. We asked His protection and care with complete abandon."[3] Like Grace, who stood soaking wet in our hallway, we all must begin by saying, "This is all I can do. I need help."

PAUSE

For thus says the One who is high and lifted up,
  who inhabits eternity, whose name is Holy:
"I dwell in the high and holy place,
  and also with him who is of a contrite and lowly spirit,
to revive the spirit of the lowly,
  and to revive the heart of the contrite." (Isa. 57:15)

Jesus, the Poor in Spirit

Jesus knew that surrender was the beginning of the blessed life, the foundation of the Beatitude Community. It is why his first blessing is reserved for the poor in spirit and why he continually stresses that we can only gain the new life by laying down the old: "Whoever finds his life will lose it, and whoever loses his life for my sake will find it" (Matt. 10:39). The blessing of the poor in spirit means that the divine life is joined to this humble, vulnerable surrender—a connection most obvious in the person of Jesus himself. Humbly born, his life at risk from the very beginning, Jesus lives a fully human life that includes hunger, fatigue, sorrow, and frustration. He relies on the hospitality of others and puts himself and his message in the hands of untrustworthy friends and followers. He does not seek glory for himself but constantly points to the Father. The climax of his mission looks like abject failure from any reasonable human perspective. Yet the cross is the truest revelation of God's character, though it is the last place we expected to find God.[4]

Jesus wants to share his kingdom with us, his younger brothers and sisters, but this means we must be united with him in his poverty. Now, Jesus's poverty is different from ours in that he really is sovereign over all creation, and we just think we are. Jesus had the right to say, "I got this," but instead he "endured the cross, despising the shame, and is seated at the right hand of the throne of God" (Heb. 12:2). He made himself poor and vulnerable to open the way for us to be joined with him in the richness of his divine life (2 Cor. 8:9). Our participation in this life comes through the practice of humility, which is our way of sharing the mind of Christ and participating in the Spirit (Phil. 2:1–11). This lens of humility helps us to read Scripture in a new light. Jesus's teaching on the sheep and the goats in Matthew 25:31–46 is often used to impress upon Christians the need to care for the poor, the prisoner, and the sick. Well and good, but what if we read that passage from the posture of powerlessness? Matthew's community were displaced, impoverished, under threat of persecution, and dependent on the hospitality of their neighbors. What if the "sheep"—who do not seem to know Jesus—were those who received these poor Christians and visited them while sick or in prison? What if "the least of these" are the poor followers of Jesus? A church that is poor and vulnerable will find it easier to understand union with Christ (*theosis*) and the hunger to know him more (*epektasis*). The gospel is also well-communicated through this lowly position, as neighbors encounter Christ by caring for his brothers and sisters. The same point is suggested in Matthew 10 when Jesus sends out his disciples without money, food, or extra clothes. They are to rely on the hospitality of people of peace for their needs, and those who receive the disciples in their poverty receive Christ.

This kind of blessed poverty and weakness is difficult for the Western church to understand. We have become addicted to the power and privilege we have enjoyed for centuries and are suffering withdrawal symptoms as it is being taken away. But while it is painful, it is ultimately good for us to let these things go. It may help us discover once again what it means to be joined with Jesus as the poor in spirit.

PAUSE

"Wherever there is humility, there is the scent of Christ, the fragrance of God."[5]

Death to the Self

Beatitude Community seeks to challenge and enable everyone to unite with Jesus in his blessed poverty. This begins by gaining awareness of how poor we really are. The poor in spirit are the ones Jesus refers to when he says, "Those who are well have no need of a physician, but those who are sick" (Matt. 9:12). They are the ones who are willing to admit their desperate need of help. Martin Luther writes bluntly, "God accepts only the forsaken, cures only the sick, gives sight only to the blind, restores life only to the dead, sanctifies only the sinners, gives wisdom only to the unwise. In short, He has mercy only on those who are wretched."[6] Dying to the demands of the self is a principle found in both Alcoholics Anonymous literature and the traditions of the church. Saint Macarius advises that good fruit cannot be produced by those who rely solely on their own efforts.[7] Catherine of Genoa insists that we must give over the care of ourselves to God, the only One who can truly defend us.[8] C. S. Lewis writes:

> The more we get what we now call "ourselves" out of the way and let Him take us over, the more truly ourselves we become. . . . The very first step is to try to forget about the self altogether. Your real, new self (which is Christ's and also yours, and yours just because it is His) will not come as long as you are looking for it. It will come when you are looking for Him. . . . Give up yourself and you will find your real self. Lose your life and you will save it. Submit to death, death of your ambitions and favourite wishes every day and death of your whole body in the end: submit with every fibre of your being, and you will find eternal life.[9]

This is obviously not easy. Dorothy Day, cofounder of the Catholic Worker Movement, which formed communities of and for the poor around the world, had a devil of a time learning surrender. During her first stint in jail, when she was not yet a believer, the only thing she had to read was the Bible. Even though it gave her great comfort, she confesses, "My pride was fighting on. I did not want to go to God in defeat and sorrow. I did not want to depend on Him. I was like the child that wants to walk by itself, I kept brushing away the hand that held me up."[10] There is a great illustration of this insistence on independence in the television medical drama *House*. Dr. House's addiction to pain pills causes chaos in every sphere of his life, so he is forced to participate in a Narcotics Anonymous group. As part of step 2 he accepts that André the Giant is a higher power than him, and maybe even that André's ghost has his back, but he still refuses to surrender his will to anyone but himself.[11] Our pride is a terrible master. Even as children we struggle and strain against the surrendering of our will. My mother loves to tell how as a toddler I insisted on climbing the stairs without any help, even though I sometimes fell and bashed my head. "I do it myself!" was my rallying cry. Little has changed over the years.

I still struggle to surrender. The surface-level addictions that I contend with—unhealthy eating, lust, anger, workaholism, isolating myself—are masks for my deeper attachment to control. I feel the need to control people's perceptions of me, to exert control over my living and work space, to have control in my relationships with my wife, my children, my friends, and my church. This does not stem from any childhood trauma or abuse but from a general sense that I am not good enough, that *I* am not enough. This attempt at control, accompanied by anxiety, is ferociously difficult to yield because it makes me feel safe in an unsafe world. Any threat to this delusion of safety tempts me to dig in my heels and control even more, or to flee to an environment that I find more manageable. These are responses I have been learning to name and surrender. This means I acknowledge that this is how I have learned to deal with my fear of not being in control, to the extent that these have become my default actions and habitual behaviors. I further acknowledge that they have not proven helpful in confronting and processing my pain and fear but have instead caused further harm to myself and to others. My pain and fear still exist, but they get buried under layers of distraction, false trails, and false comforts. I even name the voice of shame that regularly circles through my thoughts telling me what a bad and worthless person I am for feeling pain and for running to my habits. I consciously choose to reject and rebuke that voice as unhelpful and accusatory. Once these things are all uncovered and named to the best of my ability, I take it all and admit that it is too big for me to overcome on my own. This allows me to honestly ask for help from God and from my community. Sometimes this involves being affirmed and healed in my brokenness, and other times this requires being shown my need to repent of sinful and harmful behaviors. It is both a vulnerable confession of weakness and a faith-filled conviction that I do not have to be stuck in an endless spiral of hopelessness. This is how I am learning to surrender, and it is working, though the well-worn grooves have not completely disappeared.

It is not just stubbornness that makes this poverty of spirit difficult. Poor in spirit is the opposite of the modern ideal of forging your own meaning and identity. If our worldview forbids any transcendence or supernatural personality, then it is left to us as individuals to be the arbiters of our reality, our identity, our truth, our future, and our ultimate meaning.[12] At every turn we are told to "be ourselves," though we have no idea who we are or whether the identity we have chosen is a good thing to be. This makes it so much more difficult for us to come to the necessary place of surrender. Why should we? We believe, at least on the surface, that there is absolutely nothing wrong with us, because the word *wrong* implies an outside standard that we cannot allow. Deep down we may know that something has gone terribly awry, but we have plenty of distractions and enough affirmation to believe that even our sins are just personality traits.

The effects go further than self-delusion, however. We fear meaninglessness. But if we are the creators of our own meaning, then there is immense pressure to fill the "existential vacuum" within us to give our lives purpose.[13] These inner fears and pressures are reflected in the way we structure our political and economic decisions and systems.[14] So we have created a consumeristic culture of self-obsession without accountability, one that tells us we are all-important and that our choices matter, but that limits our real decision-making to options that do not threaten the socioeconomic status quo. Our society is locked in an adolescent cycle of emotional reaction and self-entitlement, bolstered by the underlying philosophy that "nobody gets to tell me what to do!" And all the while massive corporations—including both the legal and illegal drug trade—profit off our misplaced and manipulated sense of individualism. It is the opposite of poor in spirit, and it cuts us off from ourselves, from each other, and from God.

No wonder this passage has been translated as "Blessed are you in your poverty; you are not shut in the false world of convention, riches, and human security."[15] There is an incredible freedom when we acknowledge that we are not in sovereign control and that our willpower alone cannot wrest meaning and purpose out of the swirling chaos around us. What we require is a community within which we can seek meaning in our relationships with the Lord and with one another. Poverty of spirit means learning to submit to God and to each other in love.

A friend of mine entered a recovery community with long hair. Part of his transformation involved listening to and taking seriously the counsel of those who cared about him, so when one of his housemates suggested that he cut his hair as a sign of cutting off his old way of thinking, he chose to do it. Some people get very upset at this idea because our culture views self-expression as the highest good, almost sacred. But my friend was not giving in to the pressure to conform; he was learning poverty of spirit and loving submission to his brothers. I know people who have confessed to past criminal activity and served jail time as part of their desire to be open, vulnerable, and surrendered. This is extreme, but I think it gets at the kind of transformation the Beatitudes call for. Following God into a new life means letting go of the false securities we cling to and trusting that our needs will be met on the other end. As dangerous as this is, far more dangerous is the thought, "I've got this; I can handle it; *I do it myself.*"

It is worrisome that this death-to-self appears especially difficult for those in the church. A young man in a treatment center told me he wanted to be part of a church, but he wasn't convinced that Christians knew what they were talking about when it came to surrender. He didn't see any evidence of it in their lives. I had to agree. We haven't learned how to be vulnerable with one another, and this is perhaps especially true of pastors. I went on a retreat where senior pastors were encouraged to be open with their struggles and sins. Few wanted to do it for fear their confessions might be used against them. One pastor said, "There is no way I am sharing my stuff here. It will be put on my personnel form!" Pastor friends of mine estimate that 80 percent of their fellow ministers are either struggling with addiction or ready to burn out from being "bone-weary, mind-weary, soul-weary." Nor are we helped by the thought that our "insider" status will save us. Isaiah's shattering encounter with the Lord, when he realized that he was not the clean insider he thought he was but rather "a man with unclean lips," should warn us against such complacency (Isa. 6:1–5). Learning poverty of spirit is a harder road for those who have more of themselves to lose. How can we learn to practice this vulnerability and honesty in community?

PAUSE

"Saint Augustine said that 'God is always trying to give good things to us, but our hands are too full to receive them.' If our hands are full, they are full of things to which we are addicted. And not only our hands but also our hearts, minds, and attention are clogged with addiction. Our addictions fill up the spaces within us, spaces where grace might flow."[16]

Learning Surrender

Surrendering ultimate control over our lives is necessary if we want to receive God's blessing and to bless others. Those recovering from addictions can help us learn surrender because they have experience trusting God and letting everything go. They know that even the smallest compromise will invariably lead them back into old patterns. Having pastored addicted men and women for most of my adult years, I am convinced that there is blessing in coming to recognize the unmanageability of one's life. I have said many times to an incredulous group of men in recovery, "Do you understand how blessed you are? You recognize your brokenness and disorientation. The rest of us are not even consciously aware of our trouble." Most people in our world never come to the realization of their spiritual brokenness because their habits and hang-ups are more socially acceptable or deniable than drug or alcohol use. Jenny, a missionary in the DTES, credits her neighborhood friends with showing her that we all generally react the same way to stress. But because she does not use drugs or alcohol, her reactions are considered normal and acceptable. When her friends act out it is because they are craving their "drug of choice" and "have no self-control"; when she acts out she just "missed a snack" and "is hungry." People in recovery tend to be more honest and genuine about their issues and triggers. Sometimes it is because they don't have the option to hide.

I ran a small discipleship group for a year in Regent Park, Toronto, that was composed of bankers, missionaries, drug dealers, gangsters, and a woman named Stephanie, who prostituted herself to support her heroin habit. She would totter into our meetings wearing dangerously high heels, her face painted with fresh bruises from a "bad date" the night before, her arms scarred from long-term needle use. Her appearance made some of the other group members uncomfortable, but if she noticed this, she kept it to herself. She was exuberant, eager to ask and answer questions, and unrelentingly honest, once loudly admitting that she struggled with lustful thoughts toward some of the men in the circle. Stephanie became essential to our Bible study because she presented a full body-and-soul vulnerability. She could not hide who she was, so she presented it to us with absolute candor and dared us to love and accept her. As a result, the love she received was pure—she knew she had not manipulated us into thinking better of her. Her vulnerability is one of the strongest things I have ever seen. It sharply and consistently challenged the rest of us to consider the ways we were trying to hide our sins, temptations, and wounds. It revealed how desperate each of us were to control the way we were perceived. Stephanie helped me realize that I am sadly able to conceal my issues: the marks of my sins are on the inside, covered by the right clothes, the correct vocabulary, the relatively spotless reputation. I can be accepted and welcomed in any congregation in the world, but I am also terrified that people will not love me if they know me. This extends to my relationship with God as well. I know, doctrinally, that God can see my every thought, intent, fear, and sin, and that he still died for me on the cross. But in the harsh light of daily life I flinch from that intimate gaze, wanting to create an alternate version of myself who is worthier of God's love. All my hiddenness amounts to an inability to receive unfiltered, unconditional love in the way that Stephanie can. Oh, that I could say with my body and soul: "Here I am, with all of my bruises! Nothing is held back! Will you love me?"

Our group's relationship with Stephanie was typical of many relationships I have had with confessed addicts; each one has challenged me to become more aware, honest, and vulnerable about my own attachments and addictions. These relationships have led me closer to the spirit of surrender that Jesus blesses. As such, I am convinced that one of the key ways for us to create and sustain Beatitude Communities is through intentional friendship with those who can lead us further down the road of vulnerability. In L'Arche communities, which gather around people with developmental disabilities, there is a well-known saying: "People may come to our communities because they want to serve the poor; they will only stay once they have discovered that they themselves are the poor."[17] When we realize we are poor, it is easier to join Jesus in his scandalous poverty and vulnerability and easier to welcome those who already know their poverty and vulnerability.

PAUSE

"We must overturn so many idols, the idol of self first of all, so that we can be humble, and only from our humility can we learn to be redeemers, can we learn to work together in the way the world really needs."[18]

What to Do?

1. *Do an honest appraisal of your openness and vulnerability.* Openness is the willingness to share what has been secret in your life. Vulnerability is the willingness to be called on it. We need both

attitudes to be poor in spirit. This is about the basic awareness and frank admission that we need help, that we do not have this under control, that we have been unfaithful to our created purpose, and that the pain and dislocation of the world have led us into attachments that are stealing what God wants for us. How difficult is this for you?

Gather some people together who know you and love you well and ask them to identify what they see you running to instead of dealing with your pain. Write down your own answers to that question as well. See if you can also name some of the fears and desires that have caused this running. How do your answers and the observations of your friends match up? I advise people to meditate often on Psalm 139 as they do this self-examination.

2. *Create an environment in which vulnerable truth-telling is the norm.* This takes a significant commitment to one another and to the truth. I challenge Christian student groups that visit the DTES to learn vulnerability from our neighbors. I start by asking if any of them have a secret sin or wound they would not share in a church setting. Every hand goes up. Then I ask if they think everyone else in the church also has a secret sin or wound they refuse to share. Again, every hand. Is there any hope of overcoming this sin and brokenness in this life? Unsure. Do they feel trapped in guilt and shame? Every hand. I ask if they think this is a good way to live, if this sounds like the freedom for which we have been set free? No, it does not. Finally, I make the following suggestion: What if every time someone speaks in church they first have to say their name and announce their greatest failing or temptation? One of the students responded, "There would be a lot of silence in the church."

Twelve-step groups are far from perfect, but they have created a culture in which everyone is encouraged to be open and vulnerable in a public way. This inspired us to include times of public confession of failure and weakness in our Sunday gatherings. The first time we tried it was awkward, but the recovering drug users and alcoholics in our midst started the ball rolling. They helped create an environment in which it was normal to admit weakness, pain, and even failure. This allowed us to declare our need for help.

My friend talks about the need for an environment in which people's pain, experience, and honesty are validated. "There were times during my eating disorder when I was absolutely desperate. I knew that nothing else could fill my need but the Trinity, but I also needed someone to talk to who might understand what I was going through. I remember a moment when I could not force myself to eat, and I felt totally defeated. I threw my bowl of soup at the wall and called a friend who was struggling with the same issue. Maybe if the church was a place where everyone was willing to share their own pain, desperation, and defeat it would help people in my situation learn to share with others in a healthier way."

3. *Begin cultivating a shared life of surrender.* Giving up our reliance on "I do it myself!" puts us in a place of deep vulnerability and risk. How will our legitimate needs be met?

For any addict to truly let go requires a huge trust in God and in the people around them. An ongoing Beatitude Community, therefore, extends far beyond what we normally consider "religious" concerns, because God meets our needs primarily through one another. The first monastic communities were founded in prayer and scriptural meditation, but they also included hospitality, housing, teaching, counseling, work, fellowship, food, medical care, and even leisure. In short, they encompassed the whole of life, the fullness of our flesh-and-blood reality.

Cru-62 in Manenberg, South Africa, gives us a modern example of this holistic, shared life. The young men who come out of gangs and addictions and into the community house cannot be asked to relinquish everything they know and then be left to their own devices. They require round-the-clock family. So together the community eats, does chores, exercises, makes furniture, prays, worships, reads Scripture, works on recovery, visits family, and has fun. There are no distinctions: they are just family, and each person has different needs that the community seeks to meet. They call this the "Onion Model" because there are multiple layers of involvement, but ultimately every aspect of life is engaged. They are now dreaming of a Reintegration House that will help their brothers continue to live as an alternative society in their broken neighborhood.

Your church may not have the capacity to offer an official program, but that is not required. This kingdom life can be lived out in people's homes. Rediscovering the art of hospitality and communal living is not easy, but it does allow a greater understanding and experience of poverty of spirit when we realize that everything we have belongs not to us but to the Lord (Acts 4:32). Discuss what it might look like to start offering a deeper level of hospitality and sharing in your home.

For Theirs Is the Kingdom of Heaven

The poor in spirit are promised the blessing of the kingdom of heaven, much like the criminal on the cross who was promised a place in paradise (Luke 23:39–43). While this promise certainly includes a glorious life in the new heaven and new earth, how do we experience the blessing of a surrendered life here and now? The answer to this is revealed progressively throughout the rest of the Beatitudes, but it is worth affirming that poverty of spirit is the necessary starting point for a new purpose and hope in our lives.

We began this chapter with the story of my friend Grace standing in our doorway with nothing left but herself to offer, far from the world's picture of blessing, and yet somehow blessed. After Grace spent a month with us, she moved to our women's recovery home. It is a beautiful, safe, and sacred space, only a short bus ride but still worlds away from what she knew in the DTES. As Grace sat down with the other women for her first meal there, those who knew her noticed she wasn't tucking into the food with her normal vigor. Instead, she looked around at this new, peaceful environment filled with warmth, love, and hope, breathed in deeply, and whispered, "I'm home."

FOUR

Lamenting Community

Those Who Mourn

Blessed are those who mourn, for they shall be comforted.

Matthew 5:4

It is impossible for anyone who has seen these things clearly to live without grief.

Michael Glerup, *Gregory of Nyssa: Sermons on the Beatitudes*

Stokkies

There is a young man in the township of Manenberg, South Africa, who goes by the name of Stokkies. Stokkies is short and very slim, does not look his twenty-one years of age, and is somewhat shy, yet his smile illuminates when it appears. Many would be tempted to overlook him, but this would be a mistake. He is kind, funny, and has a wonderfully unique way of expressing himself through metaphors when vocabulary fails him. Like virtually all his peers, Stokkies was involved in gangs and drugs, both using and dealing, starting in primary school and continuing through his teenage years. Manenberg is notoriously beset by gangsterism, poverty, drug dealing, and many other attendant socioeconomic issues. It is often portrayed as the poster community for dislocated, broken, and hopeless people and families. Stokkies looked up to the gang members and dealers who surrounded him because they could do and get what they wanted. He joined a local gang and started mugging people, eventually becoming addicted to Mandrax, tic, and crystal meth. When I met Stokkies, he had been part of the Cru-62 recovery home in Manenberg for three months. I asked him why he left the gang and drug life.

"A lady named Leigh told me about Cru-62, and I didn't want to go. But then every Monday someone visited me and kept telling me there was another way. Then my Mommy got sick and had to go to hospital. Dowayne and Tom [two workers from Cru-62] visited us in the hospital. That day, my Mommy died, and I decided to go to Cru-62."

For Stokkies, Cru-62 is a safe place, a place where people love him and where he knows the routine of morning devotions, daily chores, self-reflection, community discussions, outings, and family meals. He did go home one Sunday and used again about a month after he arrived, but he came back the next morning in time for devotions and stood outside the gate, like a would-be monk begging admittance to a monastery. Sarah, one of the leaders, asked him why he had come back. Stokkies replied, "I saw the world again, but in a different way. I saw all the death and sickness and danger that was in my old life. I know I need God's help."

Like everyone in Manenberg, Stokkies has seen a lot of death. One of his good friends was killed the month prior to my arrival. Yet when I asked people in the township how they processed death and grief, I mostly got blank stares. Death is an imminent inevitability, with no real meaning. Everyone is numb to it. But Stokkies had glimpsed something new, a way of living that did not simply slide down greased rails toward a violent and purposeless end. He had experienced something worth living for, a community where he was not simply a commodity, a God who knew him as more than just a drug-dealing gangster. This was a place where Stokkies was learning surrender and where he could truly and safely mourn, not just for his mom but also for the pain that had been inflicted on him and that he had inflicted on others. His greatest desire now is to work with Cru-62 and help younger kids avoid the path of gangsterism and addiction. When I asked him what he would tell these kids, he responded, "I will explain what drugs do. Then I will tell them, 'Come with me, I will show you the right way.'"

The Ladder

Once we grasp the necessity of surrender and poverty of spirit, we can begin to receive the blessing of those who mourn. Mourning carries on the work of surrender because it sharply exposes our inability to rule or save ourselves. Our sense of control and competency to create meaning is crudely dispelled by the cold realities of suffering and death.[1] The starting point of this blessing, I am afraid to say, is becoming intimately aware of the shattering pain and evil of the world, and even of our own hearts. This reveals that things are not as they should be, causing us both to mourn and to long for the coming of goodness and fulfillment.

Death and Humanity

To be fully human is to have dealings with death, grief, and sorrow. Sadly, not everyone knows how to mourn. Drug users and alcoholics tend to be more familiar with the reality of death than other segments of society, but this does not mean they know how to handle it any better. My friends Dave and Paula talk about the startling number of the friends they knew in their addiction who died tragically. Paula admits that she is scared to feel sad or to visit friends who are ill because she is worried the feeling of grief might overwhelm her and cause her to fall again. She uses television to numb the feelings when they appear, aware that this is another unhealthy attachment but also anxious about giving it up.

The combined impact of pain, trauma, and the numbing effects of drugs and alcohol often keep people shut off from their emotions. The men I know in recovery work hard to rediscover their emotions, and when they resurface they sometimes can't turn off the flood of tears. The same numbing of emotions happens with all the attachments we run to instead of sitting with our feelings. Grief is an especially dangerous emotion to suppress, however, because mourning is not just a private event but also a social process.[2] Death affects communities. In her remarkable book, *Mighty Be Our Powers: How Sisterhood, Prayer, and Sex Changed a Nation at War*, Leymah Gbowee found a way for women who had been suffering silently under the ravages of the Liberian civil war to mourn together. At the end of already long days of trauma counseling, Gbowee gathered women together to talk about what they had gone through. Sometimes the communal laments lasted for hours. These sessions were exhausting but essential because, as Gbowee says, women are like sponges for pain: "We take it all in—the trauma of separated families, the death of loved ones. . . . But holding in that kind of misery was as crippling as holding on to rage. I had found a way for us to squeeze it out."[3]

Many of the traditions that humans have developed to process death and grief have been lost in our dislocated society. This loss has seeped into the church as well. If we neglect poverty of spirit and try to hold onto the illusion of control, we will remain entirely uncomfortable with death or sadness, which are clearly beyond our control. The result is a retreat to meaningless platitudes, justifications, or distractions to avoid our own grief and the grief of others.

We have frequently been told that our church, and especially our family, should not live in the DTES because it is too dangerous and tragic. It really is not dangerous for us: our vehicle is protected every night by the women next door, and our children have roughly fifty self-appointed bodyguards watching out for them. But there is a sense that it is not good for us to be around so much suffering. This type of escapism is something that also must be surrendered if we are to know and share God's blessing. Death is part of the world, and if people are experiencing intense grief, shouldn't Christ-bearers be there to experience it alongside them and offer hope and comfort? I am convinced we do not get to rejoice with those who rejoice until we learn to mourn with those who mourn. We cannot receive God's comfort if we are unable or unwilling to acknowledge pain, loss, sadness, or sin. Likewise, pastors cannot bring comfort to those who mourn if they and their congregations are detached from suffering. When God's comfort is not genuinely offered and received, addictions and attachments are the only comfort we know.

More Than Thoughts and Prayers

Our dislocated world is overrun by stories of calamity, and we do not know how to process them. Offering "thoughts and prayers" has become a clichéd public relations response to horrific tragedy, but everyone knows this offers cold comfort to those walking through the valley of the shadow of death. No better are the self-righteous social media posts that tell us all to #dosomething or the mass media whose role it is, according to Cornel West, "to keep public discourse narrow and deodorized."[4] We seem incapable of getting to the heart of one another's genuine pain and sorrow. Every response smells insincere, dismissive, opportunistic, or self-congratulatory and fails to inspire a commitment to accompany people in the depth of their agony.

Our culture has forgotten how to lament.

Lament is personal, but it is also a communal offering, something that engages our kinship relationships in response to grief and sorrow. We have lost most of this sense of kinship in our Western, dislocated world; thankfully it has not disappeared everywhere. My friend Danielle Strickland took some women from Edmonton to a village in Zimbabwe. While they were there a local man died, leaving his wife widowed. The group from Canada were amazed to watch the other women in the village spring immediately into action, knowing exactly what to do for their friend. They stayed beside her for three days and nights, weeping and grieving with her and providing all the practical food and support she needed. After three days they held the funeral, which was a celebration of the man going to heaven, including dancing, singing, praying, and weeping—but all as a final release of grief. This is a rooted culture that knows the power of kinship to help one another walk through devastating pain. One of the women who had come with Danielle was widowed herself and had been lost in her grief. Witnessing the blessed mourning of the village enabled her to encounter her own sorrow in a healthy and holy way.

PAUSE

"The man or woman wearing blessed, God-given mourning like a wedding garment gets to know the spiritual laughter of the soul."[5]

Man of Constant Sorrows

Jesus was familiar with grief and sorrow and knew the importance of lament. Everyone knows that "Jesus wept," but few stop to consider why. He mourns the death of his friend Lazarus even though he is about to bring him back from the dead. Why? Perhaps Jesus is frustrated by the lack of faith among his followers, but it also reads as if there is something essentially human in the act of grieving. Jesus also grieves the fate of the people of Jerusalem, wishing he could protect them from the coming storm. And he is in the deepest agony and sorrow in the garden of Gethsemane, facing down the overwhelming sin and rejection of the world he loves. Death, sin, and evil are all encompassed within Jesus's tears, which are part of his full incarnation as a human being. We can learn from Jesus how to likewise mourn death, sin, and evil.

Jesus responds to the suffering and sin of humanity not with "thoughts and prayers," but by embodying the Hebrew tradition of lament. Lament addresses God with a complaint, which may seem a little too bold for our pious tastes, attempts to motivate God to act, and ends by expressing the belief that God will hear and respond with mercy.[6] Lament could be thought of as prayer in the form of protest, using the honest expression of sorrow, doubt, accusation, and even rage. It is not passive: lament is an assertion that things are not right combined with the insistent belief that God can do something about it. The lamenter normally starts praising God's faithfulness before the lamentable situation is even fully resolved! Lamentations 3:19–23, for instance, lists a series of terrible afflictions but then remembers that God's love, mercy, and faithfulness are renewed every morning. This hope and trust does not necessarily remove the lamenter from the situation, but it allows him, her, or them to deal with it wisely, honestly, and courageously and to lend these attributes to others as well. This keeps the lament from descending into whining or an unhealthy victim mentality.

Jesus's most famous lament is from the cross, when in his agony he draws from Psalm 22:1: "My God, my God, why have you forsaken me?" It is a troubling question, as are all laments. Jesus's forsaken cry embodies every instance of humanity's pain, fear, and doubt, the very things that normally lead us toward our addictions. But this anguished scream of protest is neither the end of the story nor the abiding message of Psalm 22, which ends with a proclamation of praise. Jesus demonstrates on the cross how to pray and live a faithful lament through the worst possible circumstances.

Beatitude Communities are united with the mourning of Jesus, which means they must be communities of lament, places where people join ever deeper with Christ in his gut-level weeping and grieving over pain, death, evil, and sin. Paul writes to the church in Philippi that he wants to know Christ in the fellowship of his suffering (Phil. 3:10). Who would want to know this? Only those who want to really know Christ, who want to be united with the man of constant sorrow through picking up their cross and dying to themselves.

My friend Katie says this about suffering in and through Christ:

There are some seasons of life when sadness feels tangible, so solid that I could wrap myself around it at night. For me this is what it means to be acquainted with grief. I no longer look at it through a glass wall, hoping I can observe it and learn something from it. No, instead I come close and allow the Man of Sorrows himself to fall face first into my pain. Together we weep. Together we cry out to the Father. Together we face the next day. Together we share the gift of mourning. Jesus did not rise in a resurrected body free from wounds, but he chose to keep the scars of his victory so that they would testify to God's goodness. By sharing in his suffering we have the privilege of resurrecting with marks that proclaim our freedom in Christ.

If we don't want to know Christ's sufferings, we won't want to know the sufferings of others, not in our church, not in our world. And if we don't want to know about suffering and to learn to lament with others, then we are of no use as a church, and certainly of no use to those trapped in addictions or to a dislocated world.

PAUSE

These two prayers were left in a 24-7 Prayer room by a young woman who had attempted suicide several times after losing her sister.

> I was once in my mother's womb—
> I felt the big closeness. Yet now I feel distant.
> I don't feel close to anyone.
> I haven't for years.
> I've coped alone.
> But now, God, I can't. I'm fed up. I give up.
> I am so sick of being alone. I need peace.
> My heart feels physically tangled up.
> Twisted and torn, hurt and broken.
>
> —
>
> I ask you today to begin to heal me.
> Save me before it's too late.
> Out of anyone, you can.[7]

Learning Lament

Learning lament is the natural progression from poverty of spirit. When we admit our vulnerability, it leads to the death of things within us: ego, selfishness, clinging to old ways and the old self. These are real deaths that involve real pain, but it is a pain and a mourning that we should be glad to feel. We cannot have the true and lasting Good until we are shorn of the false and temporary. We also mourn when we reflect on past wounds or past sins—ways we have been hurt and have hurt others. I think of my friend Tim, a pastor who confessed his drunk-driving offense in front of his congregation. He had to die to a certain image of himself that had been cultivated and had to watch that perception of him die for his church as well. It was an action that brought mourning but also life as his community helped him to repent. It was an honest lament that also opened the door for others in the church to confess and mourn their wounds and sins.

The church must practice lament, must help those in recovery to lament, and can learn from those in recovery how to lament. Lament refuses abstraction and romanticism. It deals with the real, the particular, and the specific. It mourns and rages and hopes at *this* moment, in *this* circumstance. It insists on flesh-and-blood and brick-and-mortar. It *embodies*. One of the great dangers of modern religion is the retreat to theoretical prayers and theoretical answers to prayer. We do not lament well as individuals because we are not willing (or encouraged) to go deep enough into our own pain, anger, and disappointment. In this we lack courage. We do not lament well with others because we are not willing (or encouraged) to go deep enough into the brokenness of our neighbors. In this we lack love. And we do not lament well to God because we are not willing (or encouraged) to go deep enough in our prayerful, and often doubtful, wrestling with him. In this we lack faith.

Embracing and practicing lament can teach us to better love God, love our neighbor, and love ourselves. Lament requires and produces honesty and vulnerability. It creates the necessary conditions for empathy. It helps free us from the passions, distractions, and attachments that have come to dominate us, because it reminds us that the goods of this world are temporary and that we were made for something more. And it believes that the Triune God with whom we are united knows our suffering and is faithful to answer our cries. A friend of mine who suffers from bipolar disorder said to me, "I just gotta walk through more fire. At least I'm not alone. God is so powerfully near I can't even express it. Even when I'm screaming. Especially then."

The pain we feel in mourning is a result of God's kindness. Paul talks about a *godly grief* that "produces a repentance that leads to salvation without regret" (2 Cor. 7:10). This differs from worldly grief, which only leads to death, a grief we are well-versed in through self-hatred and shame. Godly grief can be described as *contrition* for having replaced God with attachments, and it is a gift. Matthew the Poor describes contrition as "a positive thing, part of the rebuilding of an authentic soul, a soul without narcissism, cocky ambition, or self-importance," all of which is about recovering our original purpose and preparing to be more deeply united with Christ.[8] Contrition acknowledges that we are broken *and* that we have participated in the disorder of the world: we do not just need healing, but forgiveness. It is painful, but it leads to a change in direction, a break from the disordered passions that have consumed our energy and desires.

What to Do?

1. *Practice sitting with sadness and disappointment.* We are accustomed to running away from sorrow, but true lament requires us to acknowledge and feel our pain, sadness, and disappointment. We can do this only if we really trust in the love of God, because meaningless suffering can ruin us. Within the surety of this love, however, it is OK to be sad, to have unmet expectations, and to flood our beds with weeping (Ps. 6:6). We may fear becoming trapped in our misery and sadness, but that is not what this blessing offers. To sit with our sadness and disappointment means developing the courage to avoid denying, repressing, or shoving our pain or the pain of the world away. We must not rush through lament to get to resolution as we are often tempted to do. Instead, we get honest about our pain, feel it, and express it boldly and fully, and then we ask for the ability to hand it over to the Lord with faith, hope, and gratitude. Mary and Martha brazenly spoke their disappointment and accusation to Jesus over their dead brother Lazarus, and Jesus wept with them before any miracles happened.

Rob is a well-known character in our neighborhood, a Tshimshian Nation man who loves to tease and poke at people, partly because he thinks it is funny, partly because he wants to test the truth of their claims to love him unconditionally. He often says he can't stand "all these Christians," but most days he can be found hanging out with "all these Christians," and he rarely misses a community dinner. Beneath his trickster façade, Rob is familiar with pain and sadness and admits to regularly crying himself to sleep. He has had an addiction to crack cocaine for some time, one that waxes and wanes, but he was frustrated that he could not seem to quit. "God, to me, you seem weak," he began during one of our prayer times (and some people in the room flinched a little). "I keep asking you to take away my cravings and my pain and sadness, and they are still there. So you must be weak or something. But . . . I know you still love me. So please help." It was such an honest prayer, so up-front about his disappointment and longing, but also filled with faith. To me it was a modern-day psalm, the kind that we need to make space for and learn from in Beatitude Community.

If we cannot be honest about our own sadness and disappointment, we will not be much help to others who are trying to process their own grief. And if we do not process grief and frustration with God and one another, we will find another outlet for it, most often through the temporary, false comfort of addiction. Take time each day when you pray to confess your lament to yourself and to God and to allow yourself to feel the grief of it, trusting that God is with you.

2. *Hear the lament of others.* Union with Christ means becoming well-acquainted with sorrow. But one of the great dangers of ministry among addicts is growing numb or hard-hearted. Tears and mourning help to break through the numbness and soften the heart. We started setting aside time in our church meetings to listen to one another's pain, sorrow, doubt, and even anger before God. And then, like Job's friends (before they got all preachy) we take time to weep alongside one another or to respond with holy, faithful, compassionate fury or with deep, body-racking sobs and cries. There are times when we even dare to scream "Enough of this!" This requires faith that God is not intimidated by our honesty and vulnerability. But this needs to extend beyond Sunday morning gatherings. Sorrow can be heard at the dinner table, over coffee, in prayer, and during late-night conversations because mourning is a process, not an event. It keeps returning to us, and we need people who can listen to us, stay with us in our grief, and keep us from running to our numbing distractions. We must, of course, acknowledge that people who have suffered long may not wish or even need to continually relive their painful story through the telling. Many recovering drug users become known in Christian circles for their heartbreaking journeys, and constant public repetition can lead to a dangerous mixture of pedestaling and voyeurism. Our pain should be shared, but carefully, wisely, and accountably. This is an important corrective to a culture that encourages us either to sensationalize our stories or to internalize and privatize our mourning.

My friend Al McKay regularly visits people in the neighborhood, bringing soup and poems. He listens to everyone's stories, hopes, and laments, and he holds them all deeply in his heart. Every December he hosts "Blue Christmas" events that give voice and ear to people's laments at the culmination of the year. The crux of this event is the reading out of names, situations, and painful losses that are acknowledged and mourned. Here is part of the script he has written:

> A Blue Christmas event or ceremony recognizes the tensions and pain we feel at Christmas and tries to create an experience of releasing this tension to the Creator, who walks with us in our deep sadness over the losses of friends and family, jobs, relationships—the burdens we carry of mental illness, addictions, and generational trauma. This Blue Christmas is rooted in the messiness of the first Christmas, which gives us a point of contact with the messiness we find in our own lives. I believe the tension and sadness we experience is part of the original story of Christmas. My belief is that it is better to be with others and to share our feelings than to sit alone in our rooms. Come together and experience the sadness and the hope of a Blue Christmas.

3. *Accompany one another honestly, faithfully, and hopefully in lament.* Beatitude Community requires the kind of commitment to one another that is considered foolish in our world. But if we ask people to surrender their addictive comforts, we had better be present in the very real and ongoing sorrow they will experience. When Nehemiah hears of the disgrace and danger of the people living in Jerusalem, he doesn't start by making plans or raising funds. First, he mourns, fasts, and prays, taking their pain into himself. William Booth's advice to missionaries was likewise "Try tears."

Navah Church in Kansas City has been learning this the hard way. Over the past few years, this community has weathered waves of pain and loss, culminating in two of their leaders, Katie and Jason, learning that their child had stopped moving in the womb. After an emergency C-section, little Benjamin was born without any brain function. He died eight days after birth, and no explanation was found for his condition.

During these eight days Katie, Jason, and Benjamin were held in people's hearts around the world. They freely offered their pain and vulnerability to their community, and Katie testifies that Benjamin mobilized more prayer in eight days than she had managed in eight years as a prayer missionary. But it was more than just thoughts and prayers. Their community shared their grief. Katie says, "As a trained counselor I practice saying phrases like, 'I have no idea what it's like to be in your shoes,' or 'I can't begin to understand your situation.' But in the dark, guttural places of pain I thought, 'No. You can relate to my pain, and I can relate to yours. We are all familiar with suffering.'" It was in this time, she confesses, that she began to experience "the oneness of all of creation groaning, longing for a heavenly perfection that often remains elusive. . . . Within hours of losing Benjamin I found that my pain was not my own. It was part of a collective whole, an entire race of broken, hurting, longing people. And due to some strange, mysterious, grace of God, that struck me as beautiful. I was not alone."

This was nevertheless far from an easy walk, and self-protection, pride, and deflection still tempted them away from vulnerability. The church, reeling from the repeated blows of sickness and death, wondered if they had the strength to carry on. Yet their corporate commitment to lament and to being honest about their discouragement eventually . . . slowly . . . painfully opened the door to renewed worship, prayer, and healing. They carried one another, just as Christ was carrying them all, and they began to experience miracles in their midst. Katie found that when she resisted the temptation to run from her grief or to hide her grief from others, "it acted in me like a refining fire, burning away everything but Christ."

I asked Katie specifically about how the blessing of mourning might help someone overcome addiction:

> I believe the enemy knows how powerful and effective the refining fire of suffering can be to a believer. It is a ticket to intimacy with the Lord, to supernatural strength and grace that then perplexes the world. Vices such as alcohol, Netflix, social media, narcotics, etc. all have the same effect. They numb the pain that seeks to draw us toward God. Seasons of suffering are ripe for redemption. We do ourselves no favors by quieting the cries of grief to temporarily relieve the pain. How good it is when brothers dwell together in unity through rejoicing

and wailing, through tears of suffering and shouts of hallelujah. A community that has learned the blessedness of mourning together will manifest the pure gospel of hope to a broken and hurting world.

For They Shall Be Comforted

Remember that lament is not just a complaint; it is a *faithful* complaint. It assumes that God hears our cry and that we can receive his help. This is not to say that all our difficulties will be resolved as we think they should. Making *that* empty promise is one of the worst things that we can do. Rather, in the act of lament we are given hope and perspective through the knowledge that Jesus and others are walking alongside us. Lament teaches us that shared pain is somehow eased and shared joy is magnified. Lament is not despair; it is careful observation of a fallen world matched with an appropriate response, a response that helps clear the way for the possibility of comfort and joy. I know many people who seem satisfied to wallow in the identity of brokenness, woundedness, and even sinfulness. They agree that God accepts them in their mess but have forgotten that Jesus says, "In the world you will have tribulation. But take heart; I have overcome the world" (John 16:33). Jesus is not only compassionate but also mighty to save. We need to sit in our sorrow and hear one another's lament, but we do not need to remain in helplessness and hopelessness. We are promised that the blessing of mourning is attached to the blessing of comfort.

When our friend Bee asked to meet with my wife and me, we knew something serious was up. We had known and loved Bee from her early teenage years. Her life and her family's life had followed an intermittent pattern of substance-use disorder, stemming from the trauma of war on her father's side and the trauma of Canadian Residential Schools on her mother's side.[9] Bee grew up fearing abandonment and rejection but found that drinking and sex helped her feel like she fit in and pleased others. Her life had changed substantially, however, and she was exploring a new relationship with a good, godly man. Then, to her shock, she discovered that she was pregnant from a previous relationship. Still a teenager, she did not think she could parent the child herself. Would my wife and I consider raising the baby?

We said, "Of course," and promised to support her through the whole process. A week later, however, an ultrasound found something wrong with the amniotic fluid in the womb, meaning the baby's lungs would not develop. Bee was repeatedly advised by doctors to terminate the pregnancy, but she held onto the hope that a miracle could happen and insisted on delivering her child. When the moment finally came, twenty people from our community gathered in the hospital to pray and believe alongside her. A little girl was born, alive, but not breathing well. It seemed clear that she would not live long, but we prayed, sang, wept over her, and dedicated her to the Lord. After a beautiful, heart-rending hour and a half, she went to meet her Creator, and we melted into lament. I have done many difficult things in my life, but none more difficult than this.

One of the nursing staff came over to me and said, "I'm so sorry. We just didn't know." What didn't they know? It turns out, they didn't know that Bee was surrounded by Beatitude Community. They had dismissed her as an unmarried, First Nations, addicted teenager without the support or resources to walk such a difficult road. A statistic, not a person graced with the love of family and the powerful Spirit that resides within her. Nobody should be dismissed, no matter what their life situation. This is the broken kingdom of assumptions and prejudice at work, but it was resisted with communal lament.

At the funeral we saw something of the miracle we had been praying for, as old rifts and wounds within Bee's family began to be salved with the tears of mourning. There was a deep unity of shared pain and tears forged in the family and with the community. The great gift of lament was honesty and vulnerability, along with the perspective that something even bigger than our hurt was in the room. Eulogizing an infant is not an easy task, but in this case there was something so true and life-giving that could be affirmed: "For her entire life, from the first moment you knew about her in your womb until the moment of her death in your arms, your child was loved, fought for, sung to, prayed over, and wanted with a ferocious hope. Who among us can say the same? What a blessed life! And now she has gone ahead of us into glory with the Father. We are sad, desperately so, but she is not and never will be. What a gift of life and love you have given to her, and to us. Thank you."

A little over a year later, Bee was married to the man who had walked beside her so faithfully and compassionately through her pregnancy and grief, and the wedding was as joyous an event as I have ever experienced. We, as a community, were blessed to mourn and to rejoice together, and we learned to process together the type of pain that normally leads to distraction, numbing, attachment, and addiction.

FIVE

Contented Community

The Meek

Blessed are the meek, for they shall inherit the earth.

Matthew 5:5

There are three things all wise men fear: the sea in a storm, a night with no moon, and the anger of a gentle man.

Patrick Rothfuss, *The Name of the Wind*

My father used to say grant when he was praying instead of give because it's less demanding. Meek. I wondered if my father has inherited the earth because according to Scripture he should be running the entire show down here right now.

Miriam Toews, *All My Puny Sorrows*

Jesus Walks

If you want a compelling picture of mass cultural addiction, go to a mall at Christmas. There is nothing wrong with gift giving, but the frantic, credit-driven, occasionally violent pursuit of consumer goods, undertaken ostensibly in the name of Jesus, is a bizarre annual ritual that demonstrates the discontent of our dislocated society. Wendell Berry explains how advertisers manipulate people "by inducing in them little panics of boredom, powerlessness, sexual failure, mortality, paranoia" so that "they can be made to buy (or vote for) virtually anything that is 'attractively packaged.'"[1] We know that this will not satisfy our need for connection and purpose, but most of us participate anyway. We can't seem to help ourselves.

One year our teen group decided to address this using something called a "Jesus Walk." This involves going to a mall during the busy Christmas rush, lining up single file, and walking through the mall as slowly . . . as . . . you . . . can. I mean, hilariously slowly. The point is to confront the breathless pace of Christmas shopping with our slow-moving bodies and nonanxious presence.

People immediately started asking us, "Why are you walking so slowly?" Our set response was, "Why are you walking so quickly?" Some shoppers started filming us, others asked if they could join in. Everyone was smiling and most people understood and even appreciated what we were trying to do. It was all very fun, to begin with.

I wasn't sure how mall security was going to react to the fifteen of us as we Jesus-walked through the mall, but I figured it wouldn't be too bad. Unfortunately, I underestimated the strength of the idols of consumerism and control. Within ten minutes a deployment of security guards surrounded us, and they were not happy.

"You have to leave the mall, now!"

"OK, where is the nearest exit?" The guard told me where the closest door was, and we began walking toward it. As slowly as possible.

"Walk *normally!*" one of them screamed.

"What is normal?" I responded.

"How would you like to get a lifetime ban from the mall?" I don't think they understood what we were doing.

"How would you like to be dragged out of here in handcuffs!?" The guards were yelling at the teens and nearly apoplectic with rage at me, the leader of the supposed anarchistic invaders of their hallowed ground. They confiscated the cameras of people passing by,

desperate to suppress any public record of this apparently dangerous event. The teens were shaken, but they kept walking, silently,
slowly, *meekly*.

When we finally reached the center of the mall after about a half
hour, I called us all to a halt. With the security guards surrounding us
in a defensive circle, I asked the teens about what had just happened.
Why were these nice people so furious with you? Didn't they want
teenagers spending as much time as possible in their mall?

The answers were perceptive. "We weren't buying anything, so
they didn't see any purpose to us." "We were distracting people from
shopping." "They were afraid of us because they couldn't make us
do what they wanted."

This last answer was powerful. I had said to the angriest of the
guards, "I'm sorry you feel pressured to threaten us. We don't hate
you. But you cannot make us walk faster. We are not harming anyone,
we are just walking slowly, and we are on our way out. *Slowly*."

We learned everything we needed to know about malls that day.
But we also learned that meekness is a healthy and holy way to resist
the insistent lure of this and other attachments.

The Ladder

Learning the blessing of mourning can be dangerous, because it is
easy to become enraged with the brokenness of the world. Practicing lament in my neighborhood means hearing or reliving stories
of abuse—sometimes familial, sometimes institutional—that led
to destructive addictions and the devastation of lives and families.
We live in an outrage culture where people take to the internet to
vent their fury with practiced efficiency. I could happily join in with
a reckless display of wrath, either online or in the streets. It would
feel good to do so. But if I have learned to surrender and lament,
my response to the suffering and deception of the world won't be
driven by the heat of my emotions, my lust for vengeance, or my
self-righteousness. The blessing of meekness is the next step in our
union with Christ, and it is the blessing that helps us learn holy
responses to mourning.

Power and Passion under Control

The word *meek* is often misunderstood to mean weak, spineless, bland, nonconfrontational. It is sometimes employed to tell people that good Christians avoid making waves and accept things as they are. But this cannot be the biblical meaning of meekness. Moses and Jesus are both described in Scripture as "meek" (Num. 12:3; Matt. 11:29; 2 Cor. 10:1). Yet both get angry, both confront the major powers of their day, and neither are boring pushovers. This is important to grasp, because timidity will not help anyone overcome their addiction. Recovery takes an incredible dedication and a commitment to daily struggle; it is no wishy-washy affair.

To understand and receive the blessing of meekness, then, we need a better definition. The ancient understanding of meekness was an attitude halfway between excessive anger and excessive *angerlessness*.[2] It is power and passion under control, a firm holding to what is right, and a careful discernment of the things we can control and the things we cannot. To illustrate this, a friend of mine closes one hand into a fist and pushes it against his other open hand. There is a balance between these two postures: one is closed and firm, the other is open and flexible. If we are only closed and firm, we give into anger or try to "white-knuckle" our way through difficulties. If we are only open and flexible, then we compromise and are "tossed to and fro by the waves and carried about by every wind of doctrine, by human cunning, by craftiness in deceitful schemes" (Eph. 4:14). Meekness exists in the space between the two. In our Jesus-walk we deemed it appropriate to be angry with the way our consumeristic society plays on people's addictions and attachments, especially around Christmas. But our anger was held under control, just as the movement of our bodies and our responses to the security guards were held under control. We resisted the manipulations of the mall, but we also resisted the rage and fear in our hearts and tried to treat everyone with kindness. One of the most difficult things for people to learn as they walk through recovery is how to resist the temptations and triggers that are ever present, from without and from within. They must be firm and strong in their resistance, but not rigid. They must also learn to be flexible and calm with things they cannot control, but not slip into carelessness. You can see the difficulty.

Learning to understand and practice this balanced meekness is a key marker for success in recovery. If you need to be constantly busy or distracted just to avoid your addiction, then you have simply replaced one attachment with another. Cigarettes, coffee, exercise, new hobbies, Netflix, romantic relationships, work, volunteering—all of these and more are used as methods to divert our attention away from our addictions and from the fear and pain that fuel them. Replacement does work temporarily, and our new attachments might be healthier and more manageable than our old ones. But it is still not freedom. Sometimes people try to use religion as their new addiction. What could be better, they think? Except God will not be used as a divine dealer who exists solely to give us things, make us feel good, and keep us sober. God is our Helper, our Comfort, our Healer, and our Savior, and he absolutely does meet us in our distress with his mercy. But he is also our Lord, the disturber of our false comfort, and we must not relate to him as if he were an idol that fulfills all our wishes. Not just those in recovery hold this image of God as a genie in a bottle, and it is another attachment that must be let go if we want to enter the mystery of relationship with our Creator. We aren't free to do this until we disentangle ourselves from every obsessive need to be numbed or distracted and from every shortcut. This is why it is so important for Beatitude Communities to learn the meek and contented way of Jesus.

PAUSE

I am no longer my own, but thine.
Put me to what thou wilt, rank me with whom thou wilt.
Put me to doing, put me to suffering.
Let me be employed for thee or laid aside for thee,
exalted for thee or brought low for thee.
Let me be full, let me be empty.
Let me have all things, let me have nothing.
I freely and heartily yield all things to thy pleasure and disposal.

And now, O glorious and blessed God,
Father, Son and Holy Spirit,
Thou art mine, and I am thine. So be it.
And the covenant which I have made on earth,
Let it be ratified in heaven. Amen.[3]

Gentle Jesus?

Jesus has somehow been transformed in our collective imagination into someone who is *soft* and *nice*, which are better descriptors for a pillow than for the Son of Man. Or if not this, then a generally good and reasonable man, unjustly killed by people with an axe to grind against him for carrying a message essentially indistinguishable from our more moderately progressive agendas. We only want Jesus to be offensive toward the kind of people we ourselves feel comfortable offending.

This neutering of Jesus is strange, because there is unimaginable power that resonates even in the most obviously human depictions of him. He knows exactly who he is and what he has come to do. He challenges those who would be his enemies, such as the politico-religious elite, but he also strongly rebukes his family and friends for tempting him to lay down his identity and purpose. His refusal to react selfishly, rashly, or vengefully when confronted by insult and injury requires enormous restraint and discipline. Jesus also could never be accused of cowardice. Physically weakened, he utterly rejects compromise with Satan in the wilderness, just as he rejects any concessions to either Herod or Pilate at his trial. Picture Jesus exhausted, hungry, beaten, and bloodied but unbowed, an image that must square with our concept of meekness. Or think of Jesus hearing about Lazarus and setting his face toward Jerusalem, knowingly walking into the valley of the shadow of death, his purpose unalterable. This is meekness. Or conjure up Jesus's shocking cleansing of the temple. This is not uncontrollable rage; it is deliberate exorcism of a space that is meant for the glory of God, and he knows exactly what the consequences will be. Or consider Jesus's anguished prayer in the garden, a moment so filled with dread and determination that blood leaks out his pores. All this and more must be included in any discussion of Jesus's meekness.

Then there is the cross. The cross does not just *happen* to Jesus. It is an intentional act of holy resistance and restraint. On the cross Jesus is completely holy as he resists and overcomes the system of the world and the Accuser. He is *Christus Victor* over sin, death, and Satan even as he bleeds and suffocates. On the cross Jesus is completely open and vulnerable to the world. His victory comes through restraint: he receives abuse even as he dies with forgiveness on his lips. The tension between his holiness and his openness is literally *excruciating*. This is what meekness looks like.

Learning Contentment: A Nonanxious Presence

The blessing of union with Christ in his meekness, then, is the blessing of power under control; of courage and calm fortitude; and of the excruciating, holy tension between vulnerability and resistance to the world. Above all, it is the blessing of contentment, which can be described as having a nonanxious presence. Jesus teaches his followers to not worry but to be grateful for what we have—attitudes that are essential to successful recovery. This is not just a matter of personal devotion, but also of the way we interact with the world. Wendell Berry argues that following Christ means envisioning and working for "an economy of necessities rather than an economy based upon anxiety, fantasy, luxury and idle-wishing."[4] Meek, contented communities are trustworthy, simple, and hold firm to faith and love but do not force themselves on anyone. They know their responsibility is to be faithful to their calling but are not anxious about worldly results.

The disciples do not understand this while Jesus is physically with them. They argue over position and rank; they get annoyed with time-consuming widows; they want to call down fire on their enemies; and they are impatient for Jesus to get on with ruling and reigning. They are rash, discontented, impetuous, and incapable of even staying awake with Jesus in prayer, let alone standing with him when the soldiers come. But once they witness the resurrection and are filled by the Spirit they begin to get it. This is what union with Christ can do. Peter and John are different as they stand before the Sanhedrin and refuse to stop talking about Jesus, even when threatened with death. These inconstant followers, these deniers of Jesus, these people who melted away into the darkness when Jesus was apprehended now rejoice after being beaten for the sake of Christ! Threats, violence, imprisonment, even martyrdom—nothing can stop them from telling the truth. *Something* must have happened to them to create such courage and contentment.

Paul urges contentment as well: "I have learned the secret of being content in any and every situation, whether well fed or hungry, whether living in plenty or in want. I can do all this through him who gives me strength" (Phil. 4:12–13 NIV). This is a guy who lists shipwrecks, whippings, stonings, beatings, and a nasty thorn in his flesh on his ministry résumé. He learned contentment in his identity in Christ, which allowed him to boast in his weakness and face any situation with freedom and confidence.

Beatitude Communities are likewise to be a nonanxious presence even if or when the world starts crumbling down around us. We should hope to become like Jesus in the boat, so unafraid of the storm that we can take a nap. Unfortunately, churches have had a hard time figuring out the right posture with regard to power and contentment, which has a big impact on the way we help one another in addiction and recovery. Fear and pride cause us to grasp hold of whatever power we can get and to constantly radiate anxiety about losing what we have. This helps to explain the culture wars the church has engaged in over the last several decades, the frantic desire to continue influencing political and social life even at the expense of core beliefs. If we have not learned meekness and contentment in the face of the world's trials, temptations, and even disregard, then we will not only cause great harm but also be of no good to those who need to learn meekness for their personal battle against addiction.

PAUSE

"One of the chief obstacles to this perfection of selfless charity, is the selfish anxiety to get the most out of everything, to be a brilliant success in our own eyes and in the eyes of other men. We can get rid of this anxiety only by being content to miss something in almost everything we do. We cannot master everything, taste everything, understand everything, drain every experience to its last dregs. But if we have the courage to let almost everything else go, we will probably be able to retain the one thing necessary for us."[5]

24-7 Prayer Movement

Some of my favorite examples of this contented, nonanxious presence at the heart of meekness are 24-7 Prayer rooms. These nonstop prayer rooms tend to be situated in the middle of dislocated, anxiety-driven environments: slum hotels, prisons, party islands, gang territory, drop-in centers, refugee camps, and parliament buildings. An hour or two in a prayer room can facilitate slowing down, resting in our busyness, laying down our belief that the Lord needs (or is even asking for) our frenetic activity, and reorienting toward the presence of Christ. We remember who and whose we are. This can help quell our anxiety as we make grateful requests to God and receive divine peace to guard our hearts and minds (Phil. 4:6–7).

I have shared many prayer rooms with addicts of all varieties, and the anxiety that slides off people's shoulders when they enter a space of prayer is miraculous. It is as if they remember how to breathe. One teenager wrote a note in a prayer room at the back of a youth drop-in center: "I have tried alcohol, weed, crack, and ecstasy, but nothing compares to the high of this room." He lived a pretty chaotic life, but he would rest and pray for hours in the room. There is something about having nothing expected of you but letting yourself be encountered by God that seems to take the pressure off. It isn't laziness, it's learning contentment.

This is true for even anxious control freaks like me. I remember calculating the number of hours I had spent in our prayer room on the fifth floor of a DTES hotel at the corner of Main and Hastings. I could see the thriving drug trade on the street below our window, and I wondered aloud if I was wasting my time when I could be out there Making A Difference! That's when I discerned the voice of Jesus saying to me, "Yes, you are being wasteful. But I am worth wasting your time on." Our society's default is to be too active and busy, to try to fix the pain and mourning of the world with our frantic efforts. It takes discipline for us to stop and pray. Interestingly, many of our community's most fruitful ideas for mission and justice have been born out of this nonanxious place of waiting in prayer. Prayerful intimacy with Jesus leads to the possibility of recognizing Jesus when we meet him on the streets. We teach this to missionaries who come to our neighborhood: Instead of assuming you need to bring Jesus into the poor neighborhood, how about assuming that Jesus is already here and wants to meet you? Go out, try to find Jesus, and love him! We had one group hold a sign saying "Free Prayer" at a busy drug-dealing corner across from the prayer room. They were nervous: What if people asked for prayer? What if they didn't? Some locals saw their sign and their anxiety, approached them, and said, "Hey, we see you are asking for free prayer. We can pray with you!" They stood on that corner, sharing Jesus together in contentment, all anxiety dispelled. This is the blessing of meekness.

What to Do?

1. *Memorize the serenity prayer.* This is a prayer that twelve-step groups repeat at every meeting, so memorizing it will help you learn some language that is used by recovery communities all over the world. It will also help you ingest a fundamental truth about what it takes to stay on the recovery path. This prayer is a powerful reminder that there are things we can change and things we cannot change, and we need different spiritual resources to deal with both of those realities. But no matter what the situation, we are asking God to help us embody the meekness of Christ. Most twelve-step groups use only the first part of the prayer, but I recommend memorizing and reflecting carefully on the whole prayer as a community. When you have done so, examine your personal and communal attachments and fears, and honestly ask yourself for each one: Is this a matter that requires greater serenity on my part, or greater courage?

> God grant me the serenity to accept the things I cannot
>   change;
> Courage to change the things I can;
> And wisdom to know the difference.
> Living one day at a time;
> Enjoying one moment at a time;
> Accepting hardships as the pathway to peace;
> Taking, as He did, this sinful world as it is, not as I would
>   have it;
> Trusting that He will make all things right if I surrender to
>   His Will;
> So that I may be reasonably happy in this life and supremely
>   happy with Him forever and ever in the next.
> Amen.[6]

2. *Explore anger through a fearless moral inventory.* "Be angry and do not sin; do not let the sun go down on your anger, and give no opportunity to the devil. . . . Let all bitterness and wrath and anger and clamor and slander be put away from you, along with all malice" (Eph. 4:26–27, 31). Easier said than done, but this is vital wisdom for learning contentment.

Step 4 prescribes a searching and fearless moral inventory of ourselves, and step 5 requires admitting to ourselves, to God, and to one other person the exact nature of our wrongs. This takes serious courage and spiritual poise. I encourage people individually and in trustworthy pairs or groups to examine the unchecked anger in their lives. Anger is a powerful trigger that can take control and drive people to their addiction of choice. It is also an important clue for discerning areas in our life that are not fully yielded to God. Anger has an appropriate place, and people have appropriate reasons for feeling anger; the Psalms are full of anger, and we don't want to shut this important and honest expression down. But we should take great care against justifying all our anger as righteous: much of it probably isn't. Neither is this just about managing our anger. It is about uncovering our anger, seeing where it has taken control, and exploring where it comes from. Often we discover that our anger stems from deep fears or unmet expectations. We cannot be content while we are captured by this anger and fear. So we start by identifying and admitting the situations in which we find ourselves losing control and acting out in anger. We invite others to highlight areas that we might have overlooked. Then we ask ourselves the question, "Why are we really afraid?"

3. *Learn to be a nonanxious presence for people in their personal and communal struggles.* Each person's struggle will be unique to them. It is important that we don't make assumptions about one another's past and that we have grace and patience for each other's present. My friend Joyce is open about her fear of white men, which can paralyze her and trigger temptation to drink. As a white man, I could get defensive about that, or I could listen to her story, acknowledge and respect that her fear is very real and very founded, and try—with her permission and guidance—to be a trustworthy person in her life. In this way we might be restored together. I have another friend whose relationships with women have been negatively affected by a significant childhood resentment. Understanding this struggle can help us gently work together toward his healing. These are not excuses; they are attachments, strongholds in our hearts and minds that adversely impact our ability to think and act with freedom. If we love people and want them to be free, then we won't scorn them for having attachments, but neither will we minimize or enable their attachments. Rather, we will tenderly speak the truth in love to one another so that we can mature together into Christlikeness (Eph. 4:15).

But remember that addiction and attachment also come from the trauma of living in a dislocated society. We all suffer from this, but some communities have been on the receiving end of much greater suffering and abuse than others, and this will affect the way we journey into meekness and contentment together.

Too often privileged and powerful voices have told oppressed communities to "leave the past in the past" or "wait until a more convenient time." There is good reason to be anxious about the dislocated world we are living in, very real fears that have gone deep into people's hearts. We should never reinforce the historical and cultural amnesia that makes the broken system "work." Instead, Beatitude Communities must learn to acknowledge oppression without getting defensive, and humbly follow the lead of suffering peoples.

Communal struggles are difficult, and churches are wary about getting involved in thorny political situations. We don't want to react rashly out of anger or fear; neither do we want to simplify complex issues or demonize enemies. But this does not give us the right to excuse ourselves from systemic injustices or to use the all-too-typical Christian deflection "I need to pray about it," when we are actually too scared or disengaged to take a stance. That is not meekness, it is cowardice; it is not love, it is apathy. Meekness does not mean acquiescence to the status quo. It means being prepared to act in the right moment, which includes regularly praying for discernment and engaging with people's struggles when they invite us to. We must learn to become ready and willing to follow where Jesus leads us, even if it means dying with him.

There are still people trying to follow this way of meekness and looking toward the inheritance of the earth. In November 2016 the call went out for Jesus followers to join the Oceti Sakowin Camp at Standing Rock, "a historic gathering of tribes, allies and people from all walks of life standing in solidarity to halt the Dakota Access Pipeline."[7] The camp at Standing Rock was a literal case of the meek putting their bodies on the line to protect the ancestral territory, cultural sites, and water sources of the Dakota and Lakota people. They were facing the combined might of the American military, law enforcement, government, and oil companies—powers that could crush them without a second thought. Against all this they created a community with the following etiquette:

Please come in a peaceful and prayerful manner.
Please come prepared to be self-sufficient. You are expected to take care of yourself.
Please keep your area clean and sanitary.
Please help out to keep the Oceti Sakowin camp tidy and respect mother earth.
Please volunteer with camp chores.[8]

Peace, prayer, self-sufficiency, respect, responsibility, giving back, and a courageous, sacrificial stand against seemingly impossible odds.

This is exactly the kind of etiquette I would recommend for any person in recovery and for any Beatitude Community wanting to grow in the practice of meekness. It is the kind of environment that contends against a dislocated world and helps people to recover.

The churches that participated in the Oceti Sakowin Camp learned about determined meekness from these gentle warriors. And though the camp at Standing Rock was ultimately dismantled, they left a legacy to inspire people around the world to continue standing up. We need to pay attention to the pain and resistance of our brothers and sisters, especially when it resembles the costly meekness of Jesus.

For They Will Inherit the Earth

Inheriting the earth is a very specific, earthy promise suggesting real soil, real inheritance of land, and actual victory for those who stand firm. It is a risky promise, one that seems undermined by history, by every triumph of violence and greed, and by the brutality of the cross itself. Jesus's practice of meekness caused him to inherit not wealth and worldly rule, but poverty and martyrdom.

This is therefore an oft-mocked promise. Even the Psalms complain that the rich and violent seem to prosper while the poor and lowly suffer:

> This is what the wicked are like—
>   always free of care, they go on amassing wealth.
> Surely in vain I have kept my heart pure
>   and have washed my hands in innocence.
> All day long I have been afflicted,
>   and every morning brings new punishments.
>   (Ps. 73:12–14 NIV)

This is borne out today as the wealth gap increases, military spending continues to rise, and rapid-fire, emotionally charged Twitter responses are the preferred method of political and social communication. Meanwhile, the practitioners of meekness experience persecution and martyrdom. Telling someone in their addiction that if they were meeker they could inherit the earth seems like a cruel joke. Does this promise offer any hope here and now?

The meek will inherit the earth not because meekness is the best strategy for winning worldly fights, but because it is part of the revealed character of Jesus to whom the earth belongs. In the strange economy of blessing, union with Christ leads to both martyrdom and inheritance, and not exclusively in the life after death. Jesus rejects Satan's offer of the kingdoms of the earth not because he does not want them, but because they are already his by right. Satan tempts Jesus to grasp his own inheritance in a way that avoids the cross. Jesus knows that the only true way is meekness, through a victory that looks like a defeat. But it *is* a victory. God has put all things—every authority, every power, every military, every economy, every dividing wall, every drug, every abusive and dehumanizing system, every fear, every pain—under the feet of Jesus (Eph. 1:20–23). Meekness will inherit the earth.

Bobo is a young man from Manenberg who has a good reason to be discontented, given the violence and hopelessness that surrounds him. Manenberg was created primarily through apartheid-policy forced displacement of Cape-Colored families.[9] Young men and women here are not addicted and gang-affiliated just because they lack moral fiber, but because they inherited a social reality in which drugs and gangs make an obscene kind of sense. For most of his life Bobo accepted this reality and contributed to the chaos through his own reactionary fear and aggression. When he entered the Cru-62 community sixteen months ago, they witnessed his occasional bursts of anger and threats of violence. They also created a nonanxious space for him to shine a light on the reasons for his pain and anger—a luxury he did not have in a world of day-to-day survival. Bobo says he must choose every single day to surrender to God and stay in Cru-62, and the choice is sometimes a struggle. Previously he had lived a life doing exactly as he pleased, something he had to yield and exchange for a life of responsibilities and accountability. He is employed by the community's carpentry business, where he is learning to live quietly, mind his own affairs, and work with his hands (1 Thess. 4:11–12). He compares working with the wood to the work being done on his heart: slow and steady, not anxious or impulsive, because quick, ill-considered decisions lead to bad products or missing fingers when dealing with power tools. He watches both experienced carpenters and experienced Christ-followers and imitates what they do: "I imitate Pete and Sarah [the house parents] as they imitate Christ." He stays because he knows he is loved and supported by his community, who help him to become the person God made him to be. Bobo is becoming a difference-maker in his township now, helping reach kids before they enter gangs and the drug life. When I ask him what he tells them, he replies, with a glint in his eye, "I tell them how I used to live. Then I tell them how I am living now, and I say: Imitate me, as I am imitating Christ." Improbably, meekness is inheriting one small part of the earth through Bobo.

SIX

Ordered Community

Those Who Hunger and Thirst for Righteousness

Blessed are those who hunger and thirst for righteousness, for they shall be satisfied.

Matthew 5:6

Because we lack a divine Center our need for security has led us into an insane attachment to things. We really must understand that the lust for affluence in contemporary society is psychotic. It is psychotic because it has completely lost touch with reality. We crave things we neither need nor enjoy.

Richard J. Foster, *Celebration of Discipline: The Path to Spiritual Growth*

Orientation

You can always find north in Vancouver. The city is framed by mountains that loom over the North Shore, so if you get lost you can easily look up to the hills and reorient yourself. When I moved from Vancouver to places that were sadly bereft of mountains, I was constantly disoriented. People would tell me to go west or east, but I had no fixed point to make those directions obvious. I presume the citizens of these mountainless cities have their own geographical reference points, but I found them difficult to identify and use. Having been guided by the very bones of the earth, it is hard to be satisfied with anything less.

I knew one teenager who was as spiritually and emotionally disoriented as I could imagine. I encouraged a group he was in to draw pictures of themselves as if in a mirror. How did they see themselves? What might God see? He produced a surprisingly well-rendered portrait of his face broken into shattered pieces. He drew this, he said, because he had no idea who he was. He had been orphaned at a young age and had been running with gangs for a long time, using and selling drugs, committing acts of violence, not thinking about the day before or the day ahead. He suspected this was not all there was of life, but he knew no other way. "I don't know right from wrong. No one has ever told me. No one has ever shown me." This young man had no reference point, no way of discerning what leads to life and what leads to death. He just acted on impulse with no coherency or direction, a danger to himself and to others. And there are millions like him in our world. Vancouver itself, considered one of the most livable and desirable cities in the world, also ranks as one of the unhappiest cities in North America, primarily because people are alienated from each other and do not know where or how to belong. Where are the mountains that can help orient us toward hope and meaning?

The Ladder

Poverty of spirit and mourning are blessings that strip the brokenness of the world away from us. Meekness stabilizes us on a solid rock. Now the blessing of hungering and thirsting after righteousness begins our movement outward and forward toward hope, meaning, and God's loving order. This transition reflects the moment in recovery when people gain stability and begin to seek good order in their lives and the world around them.

Learning to Order Our Days Aright

The family home is meant to be a place where hope and meaning are founded for individuals and communities. The opposite of this is the personal and societal experience of homelessness, which represents injustice, vulnerability, and disruption. If a member of your family was homeless, you would probably do whatever you could to bring them into the safety of your home. But what if your home was chaotic and unsafe? What if it offered only the same vulnerability and uncertainty that existed outside your home? Many homeless people choose to sleep outdoors rather than in shelters because they prefer the disorder they know to the disorder they don't.

Addiction can be chaotic, disordered, and dangerous. It is revealing that prior to God's creative act in Genesis, the world was "without form and void, and darkness was over the face of the deep" (Gen. 1:2). Nowhere in Scripture are formlessness, void, or darkness described as good things. God's creation brings order and life into the disordered darkness: "Let there be light!" This is still the mission of the church today. We need homes and people who are committed to love, justice, and righteousness; places where we can safely detoxify from our personal and societal disorder and learn how to orient ourselves toward God. To be very clear, this is not a longing for the "good old days" (when were they?); an argument for more middle-class families and homes; or an appeal for the imposition of a static, top-down social organization, be it political or cultural, secular or religious. It is a call to reorient our sense of what an ordered life looks like and to stop putting our trust in things that provide only the semblance of safety and security. The blessing offered in this Beatitude is that our deepest desire for goodness and order can be satisfied only in relation to Christ. Order is therefore less of a model for life and more of a map that directs us toward Jesus and toward his freedom and love. But if the church, which should theoretically be able to offer a multitude of ways into this relationship, is every bit as disordered and directionless as the world, then why would people want to come in? Why would we even invite them in until love, justice, and righteousness are established in our own house?

Disordered Desires

James 4:1–3 perfectly describes the "disordered desires" that lead
to dissatisfaction, addiction, and strife: "What causes quarrels and
what causes fights among you? Is it not this, that your passions are
at war within you? You desire and do not have, so you murder. You
covet and cannot obtain, so you fight and quarrel. You do not have,
because you do not ask. You ask and do not receive, because you ask
wrongly, to spend it on your passions."

The immense energy that goes into serving our addictions and
attachments is all about warring or misspent passions. Saint John of
the Cross taught that if our passions remain unconquered by God's
love and untamed by self-control, they will attach themselves to anything and everything, and will destroy us.[1] This happens when we
hunger and thirst after things that don't satisfy. Once again, opioids
and other substances that people normally associate with "drugs
of choice" are not evil in and of themselves. The problem is when
our desires toward them, or toward any of our personal or societal
attachments, come to occupy an illegitimate place in our hearts and
minds. The desires driving our addictions are legitimate, but if directed toward unfulfilling ends, they can kick off a dangerous spiral.
We are likely all familiar with the wretched guilt and shame that
arises when we repeatedly succumb to a behavior we know is harmful
or sinful. We find ourselves trapped in what feels like an inescapable
predicament, unable to free ourselves from passion's grasp, promising
again and again to amend our lives and yet breaking those promises
ever anew. These broken promises harm us in three significant ways:
they fail to meet our real needs, they heighten our shame, and they
powerfully reinforce the psychological attachment we have to our
addiction. We are not free and cannot help anyone else find freedom
if this is how we are living.

We seem to have lost the sense of an ordered way, inside and out.
There are certain obvious causes for this disorientation, such as the
trauma of war or abuse, the loss of loved ones, emotional incon-
sistency from parents. But there is also a general dislocation that is
common to a culture that cultivates disordered desires and misspent
passions. We live in an age in which we contemplate fatalities in the

range of "megadeaths"; where we keep humans in cages on detention islands and separate children from families for the "crime" of being refugees; and where we wreak widespread environmental havoc in the name of efficiency, comfort, and profit. Kathryn Tanner highlights the real human costs of a system that elevates marketplace organization above all else: "Self-esteem plunges among the unemployed, communities and their established ways of life are torn apart, families are broken up; people suffer from grief, loss, anger, and anxiety. Even if some people are fortunate enough not to experience any of this directly but simply watch it happening to others, confidence in the moral rectitude of their lives is easily shaken or moral callousness to the plight of others ensues."[2]

David Bentley Hart connects the disorder of the age with the corroding of the human imagination, which is "the wellspring of desire, of personality, of character."[3] If the well is being constantly permeated and shaped by passive entertainment; saturated with noisy, empty nonsense; and desensitized by increasingly graphic portrayals of violence and sexual depravity, then can we wonder about the displacement of our hearts and our society? Add to this the constant push and desire to acquire more and to find a better life through material success, and you have a disastrous recipe for depression and anxiety, the modern emotional equivalents to the common cold. Alexandr Solzhenitsyn warned that "active and tense competition fills all human thoughts without opening a way to free spiritual development."[4]

These disordered desires do not simply obstruct our own personal spiritual development; they also lead to catastrophic harm for others. The ubiquitous use of pornography gives a clear example of a "personal issue" that is better understood as disordered injustice. Pornography is a $97-billion-a-year industry, with over 5.5 billion hours consumed on the world's largest porn site.[5] The average church member and church pastor is as likely—or even more likely—as anyone to be addicted to porn.[6] The typical church approach to this issue is one of personal discipleship and accountability, which is necessary but still only a small part of the issue. Porn is part of the global sex trade: a survivor survey reveals that almost half of all sex trafficking victims had pornography made of them while they were being trafficked.[7] Porn shapes the way consumers view sex, particularly the way men view women and children. Consumption of pornography has been linked to men hiring prostitutes and to the increased likelihood of verbal and physical aggression.[8] Child sexual exploitation is one of the fastest growing businesses online, with over 624,000 child pornography traders in the United States alone. An organization called REED (Resist Exploitation, Embrace Dignity) argues that we need to engage porn not just as an issue of "a man's personal struggles with temptation," but as "global injustice and abuse of women and children."[9] REED has discovered that when porn is approached as a social issue and a justice issue, and not just a personal issue, it can result in a powerful by-product: many people who are addicted to porn find personal freedom when they learn to see women and children as *people* rather than objects and to recognize their own complicity in their exploitation. Seeing the unrighteous disorder of the world around us, realizing how we have contributed to it, and encountering the other as truly human can prompt us to seek the righteous ordering of our own hearts.

PAUSE

Come, everyone who thirsts,
    come to the waters;
and he who has no money,
    come, buy and eat!
Come, buy wine and milk
    without money and without price.
Why do you spend your money for that which is not bread,
    and your labor for that which does not satisfy?
Listen diligently to me, and eat what is good,
    and delight yourselves in rich food.
Incline your ear, and come to me;
    hear, that your soul may live;
and I will make with you an everlasting covenant,
    my steadfast, sure love for David. (Isa. 55:1–3)

Union with the Righteous Brother

How do we overcome such disordered worldviews and reorient our gaze toward Christ? Christ is the mountain to whom we look for guidance, the home where we can feel safe, the teacher who shows us the ordered way. Each relationship with Christ is unique; we won't all look alike in our pursuit of righteousness and order. Yet there are some common threads to this hungering and thirsting. Disciples through the ages have discerned a threefold process for joining Christ in the ordering of our lives: purgation, illumination, and union.

We start by remembering that union is both the end goal and the necessary starting point of this journey. We are drawn up into the life of Christ first and foremost by his offer, not by our own efforts. All our participation has its source in Christ's welcome to us, and it only makes sense in the light of his full humanity and divine righteousness.

One of the most strangely essential lines of Scripture is found in Matthew 4:2: "And after fasting forty days and forty nights, he [Jesus] was hungry." Well, yes. Does this need to be said? It does, because we are frequently tempted to forget how completely human Jesus was. He knows our hunger and thirst in his own body and is familiar with all our desires. Jesus's perfection stems not from his disregard for the body or from immunity to human passions, but from directing all his desires toward their true and proper end: right relationship with the Father, with others, and with creation. We struggle today with this word *righteousness* because so often in our words and actions we add the word *self* to it. But self-righteousness is the opposite of what we are concerned with here. Jesus's righteousness is found in his love of the Father above all else. When his disciples urge him to eat, Jesus says to them, "My food is to do the will of him who sent me and to accomplish his work" (John 4:34). This loving submission grounds and orients all of Jesus's life and ministry. He knows whose son he is, and he knows that he is loved, so he knows how he is called to live. It is precisely this identity that is tested by the Accuser in the wilderness, and it is our identity in Christ that the Accuser continues to attack today.

Declaring and demonstrating that this identity in Christ is real and available for everyone, in the face of the world's doubt and disorder, is crucial for overcoming addiction. We need not be orphans: Jesus welcomes us into the divine family and promises that he is preparing rooms for us in his Father's house. It is fiendishly hard for people to believe this, though. An elderly man in a treatment circle once cried out in desperation, "How can I know this love? I have never been loved by anyone!" It is therefore so urgent for us to welcome people in with the righteous love of Christ, but we cannot do it until we know this love for ourselves. We cannot even deal with our own disorder and the disorder of our houses until we know this union with Jesus. Thomas Merton says, "I who am without love cannot become love unless Love identifies me with Himself. But if He sends His own love, Himself, to act and love in me and in all that I do, then I shall be transformed, I shall discover who I am and shall possess my true identity by losing myself in Him."[10]

Jesus challenges us, "Do you want this righteousness more than a starving man wants bread? More than a parched woman wants water? More than drug users want their fix?" We can confidently say yes only once we have encountered Jesus. Not just the idea of Jesus, or the teaching of Jesus, but the person of Jesus. Meeting Jesus will lead us into greater depths and deeper desire for his presence, for his righteousness. Each moment of fulfillment will provoke an even greater hunger and thirst for God's love and goodness, which is the foundation and motivation for an ordered life.

PAUSE

"Since we want to eradicate from our heart the passions, which are like thorny roots, so that we may plant useful plants, naturally we shall toil greatly and our hands will bleed and our face will sweat. Sometimes even despair will overcome us, seeing roots and passions everywhere!"[11]

Purgation: Let It Go

Once we have been encountered by Jesus, our part in the reordering of our lives begins with purgation. To hunger and thirst after righteousness requires that we stop hungering and thirsting after other things. Jesus tells the rich man that following him means selling his many possessions and giving the proceeds to the poor (Matt. 19:16–30). He knows that our hearts lust after temporary treasures. This lust is harmful to us and to others, and it must be yielded before we can find true satisfaction in God's good ordering of the world.

If you want to see people who know what it means to hunger and thirst after something that does not ultimately satisfy, visit a detox facility. There you will see genuine pain as toxins are purged from flesh, mind, and heart. Detox and withdrawal hurts because we have come to physically, psychologically, and even spiritually crave the comfort of our attachments, chemical or otherwise. My friend Vince, whom I met in recovery, says that the initial appeal of drugs, alcohol, or any addiction is

> acceptance, connection, courage, to forget, to numb out. And at first because of the way it makes you feel, you continue to want it. But the more you use it—without even knowing it—a reaction develops in your mind and body making it change from a want to a need. It now becomes survival. And when survival is at stake we become people we don't even recognize, willing to do whatever it takes to survive. Addiction treatment needs to work in reverse: start by getting rid of the need, then getting rid of the want, and then working on a new way of life that includes acceptance and connection and dealing with pain.

Many drug users and alcoholics journey through this soul-testing purgation toward health and wholeness. Should any less be expected of Christians and churches? Are we willing to detox from the disorder of the world for the sake of knowing Christ?

Purgation opens the possibility of becoming free from our warring passions and disordered desires. But there is no getting around the fact that this purgation will hurt. Gerald May describes the necessity of detox and withdrawal this way: "Any authentic struggle with attachment must involve deprivation. We have to go hungry and unsatisfied; we have to ache for something. It hurts. Withdrawal symptoms are real, and, one way or another, they will be experienced. If we can both accept and *expect* this pain, we will be much better prepared to face struggles with specific attachments. . . . If we expect comfort or anesthesia, however, we will feel more distressed when the pain of deprivation comes."[12]

We have not been well prepared for the pain of deprivation, not as individuals, not as churches, and not as a society. We have believed the narrative fictions of the West: individualism, the inevitability of progress, and the saving power of our economy, military, technology, and democracy. None of these beliefs guarantee good order, justice, or righteousness, yet we hold onto them with a desperate, addictive ferocity. To threaten a drug user's supply, or to threaten one of the sacred cows of Western culture, is to invite swift and furious anger. But yielding to disordered desires or inoculating people with false comforts only prolongs the pain and makes withdrawal that much harder. We are not doing any favors by downplaying the danger of our misspent passions or the hardship involved in letting them go. We can envision what letting go might look like for individuals, but it is much more difficult to imagine what this looks like on a community or societal scale.

The church fathers and mothers borrowed the word *apatheia* to describe the difficult discipline of keeping the mind free from all the disordered attachments of the body, the mind, and the emotions.[13] Purgation/*apatheia* allows a respite from attachments, a symptom interruption that is normally necessary before treatment can begin, much like detox. It requires us to stop giving ourselves permission to indulge in our known temptations. It also requires us to be open and accountable with others about the triggers that habitually lead us to our addictive behaviors, because once we start down our grooves, it is almost impossible to stop. Some people give up their known temptations on their own, but most need a supportive community, a lot of care, and even medical intervention to deal with physical symptoms. Purgation hurts physically because of withdrawal, emotionally because we confront the unfiltered reality we have been running from, and spiritually because we face the genuine harm we have caused to others and to our relationship with God.

Illumination: Let There Be Light!

There are two key developments that are generally considered essential for recovery: a moment of clarity and a spiritual awakening. The best scriptural parallel to this is in the parable of the prodigal son. The son destroys the ordered relationships of his home and family through his selfish, unchecked passion. But he soon finds himself utterly spent and famished, not even able to satisfy his hunger for pig food. In this lowly state he has a moment of clarity that his life is a living hell. He is not fully repentant at this point, not as we normally think of the word. He just realizes that a better life may be possible even as a servant to his father. So he abandons the pig muck and returns to his father's home. Spiritual awakening hits when his father welcomes him back not as a servant, but as his son. He is restored and satisfied with a feast that he does not deserve but that his father is delighted to give. That the father is satisfied because his son came home reveals just how much God longs for our good. The only unsatisfied party is the older brother, who has not had his own moment of clarity or spiritual awakening even though he has spent his entire life with the father. As such, the older son's response to his younger brother's return and his father's joy is not illumination, but bitter jealousy. People in recovery often feel they must prove themselves and their worthiness to be welcomed into the church. This suspicious and inhospitable attitude from the "older siblings" hinders the creation of kinship communities, which are necessary to sustain the transformative power of any spiritual awakening. It also reveals how those inside the church need illumination about what it means to be a child of God.

This illumination is the revelation of God's expansive love, a revelation that opens our eyes to the reality that none of us has or needs a special inside track to being God's children. In fact, thinking we have a special inside track is a prideful attachment that keeps us in the dark. The same blessing was offered to both brothers—the presence, love, and provision of the father—but only the one who had lost everything received it with gladness. I recall one friend reeling with shock in my kitchen when he heard that God didn't hate him but rather loved and wanted him. "That is news to me!" he cried with joy.

This revelation of love helps reorient our hunger and thirst toward its proper end, which is recovering the image of Christ in us. Righteousness means sharing in the relationships that Jesus has with God, with others, and with creation. If we really desire this righteousness, we will choose it above all other things because it is just that good! The wording of this Beatitude does not suggest that followers of Jesus are to be satisfied with just a little part of righteousness either, but to hunger and thirst after the whole thing. We are to never stop pursuing it until we are filled, happily shedding every weight and sin that slows us down (Heb. 12:1). This is equally true for recovery: it is not something that can be pursued haphazardly, not something that you can just dip your toe into, but an entire reordering of your life for the rest of your life.

Purgation, illumination, and union: these are the three traditional steps in Christian spirituality that help us hunger and thirst for righteousness. Too few people in recovery ever get to the second stage of real illumination of the self, and fewer still to the beautiful third stage of experiencing union with God.[14] The same, I would suggest, is sadly true for many churches.

PAUSE

"To clasp the hands in prayer is the beginning of an uprising against the disorder of the world."[15]

What to Do?

1. *Consider how you and your community offer a genuine, Christlike uprising against the disorder of the world.* Beatitude Communities must be not just a refuge from but also a challenge to the prevailing disorder of the world. We know that the stress of poverty and dysfunctionality exacerbates addiction because it lodges people in a dislocated space. The sharing that we see within the early Christian community in Acts 2:42–47 and 4:32–37 is not just a socialist fantasy. It is about creating an environment where people have less to fear, more room to be still and calm, and more room to be free and at rest, which allows the space for better decision-making and greater

individual and communal thriving. We cannot leave one another un-aided in the stress of daily poverty, violence, and sorrow and expect that we can all just handle it.

Many passages of Scripture can be helpful here—Paul makes several lists of disordered behaviors that have no place within the fellowship of the saints—but I recommend focusing on Matthew 7:1–5 and Romans 2:1–5. These passages help us confront the mess in our house before offering it as a place of order for anyone else. Then read Mary's Magnificat in Luke 1:46–55 to contemplate God's revolutionary and righteous reordering of the world. Meditate on these passages and then try to capture the order of your life or community.

2. *Consider how you spend your days.* Annie Dillard says that the way we spend our days is the way we spend our lives.[16] So how do you spend your days? What are your regular practices that lead to freedom and life? Are these practices creating a more just and righteous environment for you and for others around you? Are there any habitual entanglements that need to be purged from your life? Do your financial decisions reflect an illuminated union with Christ or compromise with the world? Do you prioritize efficiency or relationship?

3. *Take fasting and Lent seriously.* We accept the general concept of giving things up—the popularity of diet fads is enough evidence of this—but we get nervous when self-denial gets specific and personal. Yet we advocate detox and abstinence for people addicted to drugs and alcohol, which is a far more concrete form of fasting than most of us have ever tried. Fasting reveals how attached we are to certain things and how much of our passion and desire they have consumed. It also creates empathy for those who are enduring withdrawal symptoms. So ask yourself: What are you holding on to that you must yield? Food is the traditional target of fasting, but can you imagine abstaining from entertainment? Unnecessary or unethical purchases? Gossip and idle talk? Could your church community fast from spending on itself for a season, or from its reliance on technology? Fasting for its own sake is not a virtue, but when combined with prayer, it prepares the heart for purgation and leads to intimacy with God. Lent is a perfect time to practice this purgation and contrition alongside those who are recovering from drug and alcohol addiction.

My friend Sandra introduced Lent to her congregation, which was made up in large part of current and former drug users and alcoholics. After she explained the concept of self-denial, a man said to her excitedly, "That is such a great idea! Do you think it would be OK if I gave up crack for Lent?" Sandra took a quick beat and replied, "Yes, I think that would make Jesus very happy."

For They Shall Be Filled

We have eternity placed in our hearts, so while we live in this finite world, we will always be looking forward to fulfillment. We can foresee the satisfaction that waits for us in glory, but is there any satisfaction for the hungry and thirsty in this displaced and disordered world?

Alongsiders is a growing network of Beatitude Communities in Asia and Africa whose vision is "to equip compassionate young Christians in poor nations to walk alongside those who walk alone: to love, welcome and encourage the most vulnerable children and orphans, in their own communities."[17] This vision was born in Cambodia, a country whose hope and order were shattered by the violent orphaning of generations of children. Children in this situation are vulnerable to every kind of abuse, including the pain-numbing lure of addictions. Craig Greenfield, founder of Alongsiders, knew that his family's efforts alone could not stem this tide, and neither could the work depend on Western outsiders. Young Cambodian Christians were needed to engage the work of transformation on their own soil.

Alongsiders trusts in the power of faith and kinship to transform chaos into order. Local volunteers are carefully chosen, trained, and supported as they journey alongside one vulnerable child each in their own community. They help with emotional challenges, connect children to local churches, and assist with schoolwork. Children are given a healthy support network and an example for how to live justly, righteously, and skillfully. Underpinning the entire movement is the "Circle of Courage," which identifies and equips children in four key areas: belonging, mastery (skill development), independence, and purpose.[18]

The results are dramatic:

99 percent of the 330 children surveyed said they felt more hopeful about the future.

94 percent said their lives were better.

99 percent of the children are now attending school.

97 percent are getting regular help from their mentors in their schoolwork.

97 percent have come to believe that there is a God who cares for them.

76 percent have received material support from their connector churches.

64 percent report being taught about the dangers of drugs and alcohol.

Many of these children eventually become mentors themselves.

In 2019, Alongsiders opened an adventure camp called Shalom Valley as a place of healing and restoration for children and families who have experienced decades of trauma. These are the kind of results that change the lives of individuals, families, communities, and nations.

Alongsiders is an example of a seemingly hopeless scenario being transformed into a blessing. Children and families who were subject to the worst of the world's disorder are now being filled with the best of God's hope and righteousness. New kinship is being created. And it began because one person, then a few people, and then a few hundred people hungered and thirsted for God's righteousness for themselves and for the disoriented world around them.

SEVEN

Compassionate Community

The Merciful

Blessed are the merciful, for they shall receive mercy.

Matthew 5:7

It is just because we are accepted by Christ that we can accept others and accept ourselves.

Esther de Waal, *Seeking God: The Way of St. Benedict*

You don't demand a certificate of virtue before you drag drowning people out of the water, or the assurance that the man has paid his rent before you deliver him from the burning building.

William Booth[1]

Soy Milk and Murder

I was teaching at a treatment center on the topic of resentments: "What are the things that get us good and resentful, the things we hold onto with deep bitterness that steal our joy and keep us circling back to our addictive thoughts?"

One man piped up right away. "Soy milk!"

"You are resentful toward soy milk?" I asked.

"No. I like soy milk. But they only put a tiny amount in my coffee here. They are trying to save money by going cheap on a thing I care about. And I really resent it."

Our resentments don't have to be big to have an impact, so we talked about how he felt powerless and undignified by this withholding of soy milk and how he could prevent this from causing bitterness in his heart.

We then moved on to talk about guilt. We can be undone by resentments, but we can also be conquered by unresolved or unconfessed things in our lives. I asked if anyone was willing to share, knowing it is much more difficult to be open about our guilt than it is to share our frustrations.

Everyone was quiet for a few moments, until the same man spoke up again.

"Well," he said softly, "I took a man's life. . . ."

We all sat stunned, contemplating the moral distance between soy milk and murder. You could see that his resentment suddenly seemed small to him in the light of the guilt he harbored. The ensuing discussion centered around the importance of giving and receiving mercy.

The Ladder

Hungering and thirsting after righteousness describes the longing we have for right relationship amid the disorder of the world and our own hearts. As we continue to delve into pain, dislocation, and addiction, it is essential that we come to know the inward and outward movement of mercy. Mercy can be painful because it is another corrective to our selfishness and our dismissal of others. It is only when we recognize our need of mercy for the sin and sickness in our hearts that we can grasp the blessedness of giving mercy to others.

The Scandal of Mercy

Mercy is scandalous. Christine MacMillan, a high-ranking Salvation Army officer, told me of a visit she made to a man who was dying. At one point he asked if she could light a cigarette for him. She had never smoked a cigarette in her life and didn't quite know how to do it. He explained that she needed to put it in her mouth, turn on the gas stove top, and breathe in the first puff as the tip was lit. Two things flashed quickly through her mind: this man was dying of lung cancer, and she had covenanted to never smoke tobacco. Then a third thought came in and washed the other two away: What does mercy look like for this man? It looks like putting down my judgment and my religiosity and lighting the damn cigarette.

We all like to think we are merciful, but we also tend to have well-developed moral screens to separate the "worthy" from the "unworthy." People threatened to boycott the Salvation Army one year for sending Christmas care packages of combs, shampoo, socks, candy, and books to people in prison. The vitriol that was poured out on prisoners, and on those who dared to spend any resources on them, was bone-chilling. In some minds these prisoners were no longer human, deserving of nothing more than contempt, seclusion, and deprivation. Some friends who had spent time in jail told me it was little gestures like these Christmas packages that helped them remember their humanity and dignity in the darkest moments of their lives. But even this small mercy would be denied them if some people had their way.

The same lack of mercy is typically extended to those in addictions. Even those who finish treatment and abstain from drugs and alcohol for years have a hard time finding accommodation, work, or social circles except in places that are surrounded by the same drug activity they worked so hard to overcome. It is an effective ghettoization. Sadly, many drug users and alcoholics don't even feel welcome in churches, except maybe in the basement during a twelve-step meeting. In some ways, this mercilessness is not surprising. We should not expect consistent mercy from the world, or even from ourselves, without first seeing a commitment to poverty of spirit, mourning, meekness, and the hunger and thirst for righteousness.

PAUSE

Our glorification (ascent, *theosis*), ironically, follows the Way of the Cross (descent, *kenosis*). Dying to our false selves and being stripped of our attachments frees us to eternal life (now).

Did we think crucifixion would be pretty? In us? In others? It is not. It is often marked by weeping, wailing, and gnashing of teeth . . . yes, hell. But right there, in the flames, in our wounds, that is where Grace finds us. Right there, in the tumult, Beauty appears.

In that dark abyss, we find ourselves nailed by affliction to the very heart of the crucified God of unfailing love. And we find rock bottom when we surrender to his mercy.[2]

Lord, Have Mercy

Jesus is the embodiment of God's scandalous mercy, which is good news because we would not want to surrender our will to an unmerciful God. One of my favorite Gospel stories occurs just after the Sermon on the Mount, in Matthew 8:1–4. A leprous man approaches Jesus in his desperation, knowing that he has no hope of overcoming his affliction. His condition has almost certainly caused isolation from family, work, and the worshiping community. He has heard, though, that Jesus is a healer, so he implores, "Lord, if you will, you can make me clean" (v. 2). *If you will*. Is Jesus willing? And is he able? These are the two foundational fears that fuel our unbelief. We are afraid either that God is not able to help or that he is not willing to help one such as me. There is so much inside and outside of us, so much self-loathing and brokenness, that bolsters this unbelief. But what if we started from the position that God, through Jesus Christ, is fully capable of making us whole, and that he wants to? That Jesus wants to answer our prayers for mercy? Do we dare believe this?

The leprous man dares to hope, and Jesus's first response is to shatter cultural and religious boundaries by touching him. These boundaries still exist, though they are more hidden in our culture; if you don't know about them, then it is likely you have never been on the wrong side of one. Spending time with the poor and addicted will reveal just how deep these artificial boundaries can go. We arranged in our community for nurses to provide foot care for women who were homeless, addicted, and/or prostituted. One nurse looked up as she was gently washing a woman's feet and saw her sobbing. "Why are you crying? Am I hurting you?" "No," the woman responded through her tears, "it's just that nobody has touched me nicely in years."

When we first started meeting on Sundays there was a man who showed up faithfully, even though he struggled to walk the three blocks from his apartment. He could barely communicate, and he was clearly unable to take care of basic personal hygiene. He stank, and he would normally soil himself afresh at some point during our gathering, making it difficult for others to sit near him. I wasn't sure what to do about the situation but was stupidly proud that he had chosen our congregation. Thankfully one of our members, George, understands the mercy of Jesus a lot better than I do. One Sunday George gently led the man to the back of the shelter where we met and with his permission showered him, dried him, and dressed him in new clothes. The man came out beaming, no longer stuck in his mess and able to join at a deeper level with the worshiping community. George knows that it is not enough to just tolerate someone, because God does not just tolerate us. We all come to God in our mess, in need of mercy, and he does not just hold his nose and refrain from destroying us. Mercy is not our defense against God's anger; it is Jesus actively pouring out his life and hope for us, inviting us to the wedding banquet and making room for those who cannot repay him (Luke 14:7–14). God does not hate us, and he does not leave us to founder in our trouble. But we must accept the mercy of Christ, something that takes great humility. If we don't think we need mercy, we will never be open to receiving it.

Maybe this is why in the Gospels Jesus seems to primarily extend his mercy to those who are "unclean." After Jesus touches the leprous man, he responds to his request for healing, saying, "I will; be clean" (Matt. 8:3). One compassionate gesture, four transformative words, and the man is healed. Not "fixed," not "managed." Healed. He is then told to go and present his newly healed self before the priest—an action that would restore him into the social and worshiping community.

PAUSE

"Do not fall into despair because of your stumblings, for you should not consider them incurable. There is indeed a healer: he who on the cross asked for mercy on those who were crucifying him, who pardoned murderers as he hung on the cross. Christ came on behalf of all sinners, to heal the brokenhearted and to bind up their wounds."[3]

Learning Compassion

The importance of knowing God as mercy-giver is paramount. I met a man in Narcotics Anonymous who recoiled from his childhood notion of a quick-tempered and punitive God, yet he admitted that his own life reflected this vindictiveness and anger. It was only when he started to experience God as gentle and merciful toward him that he learned mercy himself. He is now growing in mercy through a daily connection with God. We become like that which we worship.

Drug users and alcoholics are some of those considered "unclean" in today's society, the recipients of regular and devastating judgments and alienation. They tend to be justifiably wary of religious environments and are also adept at being their own worst judges. I can't count the number of friends who told me they were afraid to enter a church because the walls might collapse on their sinful heads. What if we were known instead as accessible and welcoming to those who have labored under judgment? This means we must learn compassion, which requires attaching our hearts to misery.[4] According to Gregory of Nyssa, "Unless mercy softens the soul, one will not seek the healing of his neighbor's ills. . . . Mercy is a voluntary sorrow that joins itself to the suffering of others."[5] Attaching your heart to someone and joining their suffering is difficult to do from a distance; compassion usually involves proximity. One of our mottoes is that you are probably not in community with someone unless you can smell them. When we walk closely with someone, they stop being a project or a burden, and they start becoming a brother, a sister, a blessing. We begin to recognize that they are not just recipients of our charity but have something beautiful to offer us as well.

Our task is not to confer dignity on anyone. Dignity is inherent; a birthright. We cannot add value to that which has already been called "Beloved." Neither can we take it away. To say we value someone is like thinking we can make a sunrise beautiful. The rising sun is beautiful whether we recognize it or not. It is only we who are diminished when we fail to acknowledge it. Compassion and mercy allow us to see people not for their deficits but as dear children of God, filled with dignity and purpose.[6] Father John Sergiev, a nineteenth-century Russian priest in Saint Petersburg, would hold the faces of the people he found slumped in the gutter after a night of drinking and lovingly tell them, "This is beneath your dignity. You were created to house the glory of the living God."[7] This is mercy, because when we recognize beauty in people, we can help them see it in themselves as well.

541 Café

The 541 Café in Hamilton, Ontario, is a Beatitude Community that is learning to walk in mercy. It is a unique space where rich and poor gather together, not in a shelter, detox, or drop-in, but in a place of shared food and life. Prices are accessible, but not because the food or coffee is subpar—quite the opposite, the menu is delectable. Those with financial resources are offered discreet and life-giving ways to bless those without so that everyone can partake with dignity. Sue Carr, who oversees 541 and the Meeting Place Church that gathers there, cultivates a wise rhythm of work and community among the staff, volunteers, and customers. The core volunteers are from a wide mix of socioeconomic backgrounds, with some in various stages of recovery. The space is theirs, and they have created a careful order in how they prep, serve, clean, and host. When college students come in to volunteer, Sue suggests to them that they are learners, not experts. Their first "job" is to arrive at 7 a.m. to sit, drink coffee, and observe the work and routine of the regular volunteers before offering any assistance. One passionate new volunteer was cleaning up with a frenetic speed and efficiency. "Slow down," advised Sue. "You're messing up our pace and rhythm, and you're taking work from others." It is more important at 541 to see and be with one another than to get the work done fast.

The community has laid a groundwork in poverty of spirit, surrendering their need to be productive in exchange for relationship and the cultivation of beauty. The place is still hopping with customers though—mercy doesn't mean poor service or bad business. They have also learned to mourn together, having walked through pain and messiness with one another and others in their neighborhood. This gives them the right to hold one another accountable and to insist on good order. Drugs and disrespect are not allowed in the café because recognizing people's dignity means hoping for their best and holding them to it.

This is why the community was so distraught when there was an assault at 541, committed by a regular customer who has been known for years through his ups and downs. He is normally polite and mild, unless he is off his medication. After the assault, Sue could see him sitting outside, head in his hands, staring at the ground, defeated. Even as they cared for the victim, the staff and volunteers felt a deep sadness—a mourning—for the man outside. They knew a painful care for him that was not naive but rather merciful and costly. They could feel his suffering because they had attached their heart to his misery over a long period of time. They could also be angry about the violence he had wrought and the consequences that would stem from it, but through the steady practice of meekness they had learned to control their anger so it did not lead to sin.

There was one loud voice in the aftermath who used the incident to complain about the danger of 541 and the poor and addicted people they serve. The media picked it up because the media loves sensation and outrage. The attention cost 541 some customers, but most people could see the shallowness and illogic of the complaint in the light of the love and mercy that sustains this Beatitude Community. Mercy is scandalous and costly, but it is also the natural and necessary outflow of having received the mercy of Christ.

PAUSE

With the merciful you show yourself merciful. (Ps. 18:25)

What to Do?

1. *Practice publicly expressing gratitude.* You may be surprised at the difference a regular, intentional, public expression of gratitude can make in your personal life, in your community life, and in the lives of people around you. I encourage people in recovery to publicly give thanks for something every day, and we practice this in our family as well. Gratitude reminds us and others that there are things worth being thankful for, new mercies that we have received every day. Gratitude undermines the unmerciful attitudes of bitterness, cynicism, and resentment that fuel addictive behavior.

2. *Check your fears.* It is hard to give mercy if we have not learned to receive it. Do you fear coming before God in surrender and repentance because you suspect that God's mercy is either ineffective or inaccessible? Consider which fear is more dominant in you: Is it that your brokenness is too big for God? Or is it your suspicion that sinfulness and unworthiness make God reject you? How have these fears been reinforced through your family, church, and societal experiences? Take time each day to meditate on Hebrews 4:14–16, which ends with "Let us then with confidence draw near to the throne of grace, that we may receive mercy and find grace to help in time of need." If we don't believe God's mercy is available and sufficient for us, we won't be able to tell others that it is available and sufficient for them. Boldly bring your sins and fears before the Lord, trusting in his goodness and mercy, acknowledging that it is mercy that you need.

3. *Learn to recognize dignity and to receive mercy from others.* I asked a short-term missionary why he had come to the DTES and what he was expecting from the neighborhood. He answered, "I have come to serve the poor and the addicted, and I expect *nothing* in return." He meant to impress with his sacrificial posture, but I wondered: Why

would he expect nothing from my neighbors and friends? Are they incapable of giving anything he might want or need?

That kind of attitude usually produces unsustainable and patronizing forms of ministry that tread on people's dignity. True mercy finds ways to walk alongside while honoring everyone's capacity and agency. The number one rule of community formation is to never do for someone that which they can do for themselves. This is terribly hard for those of us who are addicted to feeling useful and charitable.

Receiving can be more difficult than giving, especially when you come from a position of privilege and power, but this is yet another attachment we need to surrender. Jesus himself receives from women who wash and anoint his feet and from Simon of Cyrene, who carries his cross. It is part of the discipline of humility to receive well from others, and it affirms people's dignity when we see that they have good gifts to give. Consider your relationships to see if you have failed to recognize someone's dignity, and try to make things right.

We have received much love, care, and mercy from our community. When we dedicated our son Noah at Crab Park, we invited all our neighborhood friends to offer their blessing as we passed him around. Those in the circle who were homeless, addicted, or in recovery were hesitant. They felt disqualified from giving a blessing. But we insisted and were privileged to see them carefully holding our child, silently mouthing out life and protection and hope over him. Fourteen years later, some of these folks still talk about that boundary-breaking moment when we all gave and received mercy through the blessing of a child.

4. *Become a mercy advocate*. Beatitude Communities should be not only givers of mercy but also champions of mercy and creators of new social, political, and economic realities that have mercy at their very center.

Saint Basil's "New City," just outside of Caesarea, is an example of mercy being placed at the heart of a sociopolitical reality.[8] Basil (AD 330–379) experienced a spiritual awakening that led him to give all he had to the poor and begin exploring monastic life around the Middle East. In the monasteries he learned surrender, contrition, contentment, order, and a simple, shared life. But instead of staying in that place of inner harmony and seclusion, Basil applied his monastic experience toward the aid of the people suffering famine in Caesarea. The Beatitude life, Basil believed, was neither just for monks nor only an individual matter. Reflecting on the parable of the rich young man in Matthew 19:16–30, Basil discerned that the issue was not just the man's personal attachment to worldly possessions, but the way wealth and want were distributed. He had inherited wealth while others had inherited poverty, but he was too invested in this entitled, unjust system to see, let alone obey, the requirement of *mercy*. He could not give, so he could not receive.

This lack of mercy offends against Christ's law of love, yet it is how society is arranged. Basil decided to arrange matters differently in his New City. As bishop, he helped create the first citywide provision of housing, food, and medical care through simple, sustainable living and an emphasis on sharing extra resources. Basil did not just promote charity but righteous order, or as he saw it, "restoring the balance."[9] Selfishness was an aberration, a disorder. Mercy, simplicity, and holding things in common was the cure. Basil believed that participating with Christ's mercy could provide the framework for a whole new social, political, and economic way of living together. At Basil's funeral, Saint Gregory of Nyssa encouraged listeners to "behold the New City, the storehouse of piety, the common treasury of the wealthy . . . where disease is regarded in a religious light, and disaster is thought a blessing, and sympathy is put to the test."[10]

Saint Basil's example shows that a merciful way of being together is imaginable. If the scope of the New City seems daunting, we can start by offering to accompany friends as they navigate bureaucracies like the tax and court systems, income-assistance or housing programs, or child-protection and health services. Your eyes will be opened to the unmerciful state of our world's systems, but your presence might prompt greater accountability and fairness, and you will be able to encourage your friends when they encounter difficulties.

For They Shall Receive Mercy

Mercy isn't naive or woolly. It is an intentional and costly decision to be compassionate, remembering that compassion has first been poured out on us. Jesus's parable of the unmerciful servant in Matthew 18:21–35 announces in no uncertain terms that we who have received mercy are to give mercy to others. Matthew 6:14–15 likewise affirms that forgiveness from the Father is directly connected to the way we forgive, or do not forgive, others. Being unmerciful denies the very basis of our salvation and identity, which is Christ's mercy for us. Withholding mercy from those fighting pain and addictions is especially galling, given that we all have our own pet attachments that we justify.

Those who are merciful are promised the blessing of receiving mercy. I wonder sometimes if we forget how transformative this is. I know many lives that were set in entirely new directions thanks to a small gift of mercy. Randy was chased out of his home at gunpoint when he was sixteen and spent the next several decades in search of family. This frustrated pursuit finally led him to full-blown drug addiction and sleeping underneath a truck in an alley. That is when a shelter worker, himself a recovering drug user, walked across the street and invited Randy to come inside. Randy is now part of a family and is a champion of mercy everywhere he goes.

Rudy grew up with gangs, a twenty-year meth and alcohol addiction, and a solid belief that this was a life he could never escape. It wasn't until Dowayne, himself a recovering drug user (notice a theme?), affirmed there was more to him than he believed possible that Rudy began to see himself in a new light. He joined a recovery community that he now helps to lead, offering transformative mercy to others who cannot see it for themselves.

Stan was not a man who would offer or expect mercy of any kind.[11] An infamous drug dealer with a fearsome reputation on the streets and in prison, where he spent more than twenty-five years of his life, Stan had been shot, stabbed, and thrown out of moving cars, and he admits to having perpetrated horrific violence himself. Fueling drug addiction is a violent, merciless, and lucrative business: he told one wealthy client that he nearly murdered him several times, but the seventeen thousand dollars he gave Stan every month for heroin was too important.

That life of violence and drugs is ultimately unsustainable. After losing everything and ending up in the back alleys, Stan decided to kill himself. But the pipe he hung the noose around mercifully broke when he dropped. Later, while Stan walked through a soaking wet alley with no coat, no shoes, and no hope, a shelter worker named Donny invited him to come inside and get some rest. Stan accepted this unfamiliar offer of mercy. It was a small act, and it cost Donny very little to make it, but it made all the difference in Stan's life. After five days in the shelter, feeling cared for and safe for the first time in years, Stan decided to give recovery a shot. He was forty-eight years old, and that was the last time he used drugs.

Fifteen years later, Stan is now a mercy-giver, his life dedicated to giving other suffering people a chance to find freedom. He manages three recovery houses in the neighborhoods where he used to deal drugs and death, and the motto he shares with everyone is "God has a plan." This might be a shallow aphorism from other people, but not when backed by the weight of Stan's experience of God's transformative mercy.

EIGHT

Contemplative Community

The Pure in Heart

Blessed are the pure in heart, for they shall see God.

Matthew 5:8

God has imprinted the image of the good things of His own nature on creation. But sin, in spreading out over the divine likeness, has caused this good to disappear, covering it with shameful garments. But if by life rightly led, you wash away the Mud that has been put on your heart, the Godlike beauty will again shine out in you.

Gregory of Nyssa[1]

In addressing purity of heart, we are now wandering off the edge of the map, and there be dragons waiting. We will have to go far beyond the safe conversations and revelations we are accustomed to in "civilized" society, and even in church. Beatitude Communities don't just help us quit drugs, they help us understand why we turned to drugs in the first place and spur us to seek repentance, confession, and healing for those deeper heart issues. Heed Paul's words to Christians living in Rome:

Claiming to be wise, they became fools, and exchanged the glory of the immortal God for images resembling mortal man and birds and animals and creeping things. Therefore God gave them up in the lusts of their hearts to impurity, to the dishonoring of their bodies among themselves, because they exchanged the truth about God for a lie and worshiped and served the creature rather than the Creator, who is blessed forever! Amen. (Rom. 1:22–25)

These words were a heart-challenge to the individuals who read them, but also a revolutionary broadside against a Roman culture that celebrated extravagant wealth, militarism, abusive sexual depravity, and rulers who fashioned themselves divine. It is tempting to draw parallels with our current idolatrous, truth-defying society. First, however, we must contemplate the state of our own hearts and examine why we have so easily compromised with the world's falsehoods.

My friend Karah speaks of the awful realization that her heart had been given over to impurity:

The Bible frequently refers to the heart in a negative light. At first that seemed incongruent with what both the world and my Christian circles were telling me about my heart being good. Upon deeper reflection, the truth of my heart's darkness became increasingly obvious. It had first manifested in hurt and retained bitterness from childhood and my developing years, later in confusion, fear, and anxiety. These eventually led to behaving in ways that denied the truth for which Christ preached and died. I spent most of my teen and young adult life engaging in destructive friendships, relationships, and activities to ease the misery in my life.

Eventually, I reached a crisis point where it was no longer possible to maintain the façade of Christianity, or even of basic health. When this crisis occurred, there were a small group of people willing to help me take a serious look at my life. This led to a very thorough examination of my heart, which was (and continues to be) the most difficult thing I have ever done. After an intense and prolonged process of examining the places of darkness, sin, and brokenness harbored within my heart, my misery seemed to deepen rather than lighten. What I saw in my life seemed unforgivable, but God knew even more deeply than I the sin and harm I had done. I did not think a heart that hard and fearful had any place in His life.

The Ladder

The pure in heart Beatitude comes *after* we have begun to engage the world in righteousness and mercy because it is so easy to get swept up again in the brokenness that surrounds us. It is where our hearts tend to drift. One of the most dangerous things for people in treatment is reentering old relationships to rescue friends still caught in addiction. It is right to want to help, but when this is done alone, or at the cost of neglecting one's own recovery work, it often ends in disaster. We need to be constantly reminded to come back to our true source and hope. Thomas Merton says, "Without contemplation, without the intimate, silent, secret pursuit of truth through love, our action loses itself in the world and becomes dangerous."[2] There is a lot of dangerous "Christian" activity loosed in the world because we have neglected to contemplate ourselves truly, warts and all, in the holy light of God.

Pure and Clean

The words *pure* and *clean* have a different meaning to people in addictions and recovery. *Purity* can refer to how much a drug has been mixed with a diluting substance, and *clean* sometimes has to do with the state of one's urine. I spoke once to a group of men in treatment on the biblical meaning of *clean* versus *unclean*, immediately following which everyone had to do a surprise urinalysis test to see if they had drugs in their system. I had to assure some very suspicious men that I had not planned my talk around the test.

How much clean time someone has from drugs and alcohol is also a frequent topic of conversation in recovery circles. Days, weeks, months, and years sober are justly celebrated at meetings with medallions and cake. Many acknowledge, however, that this can be a dangerous way to talk and think about recovery, or indeed about life. As we have seen, drugs and alcohol are primarily symptoms. It is great when someone stops using them, because they cause serious social and health concerns, but there are many other attachments we can find to take their place. Another well-known phenomenon in recovery circles is the "dry-drunk," a person who isn't drinking or using drugs but might as well be because they exhibit all the frustration, bitterness, and resentment of an out-of-control addicted life. This happens because, as Vancouver's long-time homelessness advocate Judy Graves told me, "Addiction doesn't start with drugs or alcohol. It starts with a broken heart, and a broken world."

PAUSE

The LORD is near to the brokenhearted
and saves the crushed in spirit. (Ps. 34:18)

Jesus

In Scripture the heart is not just the seat of the emotions, but the ground of a person's intellect, morality, and personality. In the Sermon on the Mount Jesus envisions such freedom for our hearts that actions like murder and adultery become unimaginable. When we harbor hatred and lust in our hearts it is the equivalent of being a dry-drunk. We may have the outward appearance of purity, but our inner heart reveals the true nature of our attachments and sin. This is the rebuke Jesus levels at the religious elite who accuse him. He exposes the wicked reality behind their pious façade when he asks them, "Why do you harbor evil in your hearts?" (Matt. 9:4 BSB) and when he compares them to tombs and dinnerware that look clean but are full of greed, self-indulgence, and death (Matt. 23:25–27). This is in line with the Hebrew understanding of God's searching wisdom: "For the LORD sees not as man sees: man looks on the outward appearance, but the LORD looks on the heart" (1 Sam. 16:7).

Twice, at Jesus's baptism and his transfiguration, the Father looks at Jesus's heart and declares, "This is my Son, with whom I am well pleased." We see the cost and the power of Jesus's purified heart at Gethsemane, when Jesus proclaims through blood and tears that he is utterly aligned with his Father's will. His intentions and actions are united in such a perfect, sacrificial offering of love that it seems impossible for us to even contemplate imitating. Yet Jesus wants to glorify the Father by bringing his followers into complete union with himself. We talk about "inviting Jesus into our hearts," but Jesus has first invited us into *his* heart, his pure, perfect, obedient heart. It is true that we bear Christ into the world through this union, but it is even more true that he bears *us* into the heart of the Father.

Straight from the Heart

I have asked people in and out of recovery how they feel about a God who sees our every motivation and hidden thought. Those who perceive God as a demanding taskmaster find it intrusive or threatening. Those who perceive God as a loving Savior or Father find it comforting and hopeful.

I think there is truth to both the comfort and the fear. My friend Joyce likes to say, "God sees all my brokenness, and he still wants me. He's so weird!" But we may have reasons to not want God's light shining on our hearts (John 3:19–20). People will sometimes go to extraordinary lengths to convince others that they are not using drugs or alcohol. The deception eventually becomes obvious, but I have seen men and women steadfastly deny what is absolutely clear to everyone else. I sometimes wonder why anyone would expend so much energy in this fruitless—and harmful—delusion, until I remember that we all do the exact same thing with our sin and shame. We don't want anyone to see the dark corners of our hearts, and we don't really want to see them ourselves. We would prefer to live in a place of self-deception, believing we are good enough because we aren't as bad as others, or as bad as we could be. But God presents a dilemma. Surface-level sobriety or piety, which may fool most people and maybe even ourselves if we are cagey enough, is not going to fool God.

With his clear perception of the human heart, Jesus challenges our understanding of what it means to be clean and pure. He tells the Pharisees that "it is not what goes into the mouth that defiles a person, but what comes out of the mouth," because "what comes out of the mouth proceeds from the heart, and this defiles a person" (Matt. 15:11, 18). Jesus is talking about religious ritual here, but the same principle applies to addictions: our attachments flow out of the pain and fear that rest within our broken hearts. This does not mean that drugs, alcohol, or any of our other attachments are good or wise to use, in the same way that Jesus doesn't dismiss the act of murder or adultery just because the real issue is in the heart. It means that if we want true, ongoing freedom and purity of heart, we must go much deeper than a change in surface actions.

Alexandr Solzhenitsyn grasped this truth while in a Soviet Gulag: "The line separating good and evil passes not through states, nor between classes, nor between political parties either—but right through every human heart—and through all human hearts."[3] This is both sobering and liberating: we cannot rid the world of evil or drugs or anything else that tempts us, but we *are* able to cooperate with God in addressing the evil and impurity in our own hearts. We all run emotional-spiritual con games, things we do to keep ourselves and anyone else from discovering the shady business of our heart. Drug and alcohol addiction are just the most obvious of these, but if you keep digging you will find them all the way down. Codependency, overworking, procrastination, attention-seeking behaviors, isolation—these and more all serve to hide what's really going on beneath the surface. The only way out is to stop the game and to let God lead you past all the noise and lies and justifications and into deep fear and unbelief that sit very near to the core of your being. We don't have to change the whole world to be changed ourselves. But we do not get to shift the responsibility of our lives over to other people, situations, or substances. We are not *just* victims of drugs, alcohol, genetics, trauma, or a dislocated society. These things are real and have significant impact that must be reckoned with, but we still bear responsibility for our own hearts.

PAUSE

"Self-questioning can never be without a certain existential 'dread'—a sense of insecurity, of 'lostness,' of exile, of sin. A sense that one has somehow been untrue not so much to abstract moral or social norms but to one's own inmost truth. 'Dread' in this sense is not simply a childish fear of retribution, or a naive guilt, a fear of violating taboos. It is the profound awareness that one is capable of ultimate bad faith with himself and with others: that one is living a lie."[4]

Learning Contemplation

Part of the genius of the twelve steps is that they don't rely on just one shining moment of clarity or spiritual awakening. To continue in recovery—as in discipleship—means putting in the work every day, and the biggest part of this work is contemplation. Once we have taken a fearless and searching moral self-inventory and confessed the exact nature of our wrongs (steps 4 and 5), the next two steps involve preparing for and humbly asking God to remove our defects. This is a deliberate, rigorous, and ongoing process, far removed from the get-out-of-hell-free card that passes for repentance and forgiveness in some Christian settings. Steps 10 and 11 involve taking regular personal inventory, promptly admitting when we are wrong, and seeking continual connection and direction with God through prayer and meditation. This is the stuff of blessing if the foundation is laid in grace, surrender, and the hope of union with God.

Perhaps we can see now why there is so much Beatitude groundwork to be done before we come to the place of contemplation. If we have not learned to surrender our pride, lament our part in the broken world, become courageous and contented, hunger after righteousness, or trust in the mercy of God, we will never be bold enough to open our hearts to divine examination and operation. Contemplation of the heart can be a painful journey, requiring immense patience, honesty, and resolution. We will not always like what we find.

We need God's help in letting go of what we discover because our attachments and fears have roots in the soil of our hearts. There is a frightening moment in recovery when a person moves beyond the clichés and mottoes they have been holding onto for their sobriety. Those things worked for a while, but they are not strong enough medicine for what's to come. It is like letting go of the edge of the pool and swimming out to deeper water. It is the transition from saying, "Yes, I am addicted," to asking, "Why am I addicted? What is really buried in my heart that I haven't wanted to see? Is my God strong enough to handle it? Could I actually become free? And do I want to?" This is the difference between being "free enough" and being "free indeed." But being free indeed means letting God scour out everything in our heart that offends, and this necessitates a much deeper yielding than we have yet known.

Everything in the spiritual and religious life is aimed precisely at this contemplative surrender, this purity of heart. It requires a complete renunciation of our delusions and an utterly honest acceptance of our heart, our situation, our capacity, and our standing before God with exacting truth.[5] This exactitude must permeate the examination of every motivation, every loyalty, every assumption, every attachment. The investigation must be meticulous and thorough, not for the sake of legalism, but for the sake of freedom and life. Henri Nouwen confesses the revelation of his own dislocated motivations:

> Indeed, how divided my heart has been and still is! I want to love God, but also to make a career. I want to be a good Christian, but also to have my successes as a teacher, preacher, or speaker. I want to be a saint, but also enjoy the sensations of the sinner. I want to be close to Christ but also popular and liked by people. No wonder that living becomes a tiring enterprise. The characteristic of a saint is, to borrow Kierkegaard's words, "To will one thing." Well, I will more than one thing, am double-hearted, double-minded, and have a very divided loyalty.[6]

Contemplation means facing these truths about ourselves and trusting that God is still able to create clean hearts in us (Ps. 51). Beatitude Community is especially important here, because when God reveals the truth about our heart, we will need other people to help us to stay on the difficult path.

PAUSE

The desert fathers and mothers developed a deceptively simple formula for contemplation. They prayed out, as often as they could,

Make haste, O God, to deliver me!
O LORD, make haste to help me! (Ps. 70:1)

Abba Isaac the Syrian said, "This verse has rightly been selected from the whole Bible for this purpose. It fits every mood and temper of human nature, every temptation, every circumstance. It contains an invocation of God, a humble confession of faith, a reverent watchfulness, a meditation on our frailty, a confidence in God's answer, an assurance of his ever-present support. The man who continually invokes God as his guardian is aware that he is always at hand."[7]

What to Do?

1. *Practice observation and presence.* Contemplation is ultimately a journey of presence and observation. It is learning to be attentive to what is true and unmediated in our hearts, in our world, and with the Spirit of God. This is increasingly difficult because our world, and especially our addiction to electronic screens, affords us every opportunity to escape from immediacy with others, with ourselves, and with the present moment.[8] We cannot contemplate if we cannot be present.

The contemplation of the natural world is an essential corrective to this loss of presence, as well as preparation for the contemplation of our true selves and God. Creation reminds us, forcefully if necessary, that we need to attend to it if we want to survive, because whatever we think of our capacities, we are still not the masters of nature.[9]

When I lead recovery groups through exercises in observation, I instruct everyone to close their eyes and be quiet for ten minutes so they can listen to the sounds that form the natural backdrop of our world. Or we go into a forest to stare at a tree for an uncomfortable amount of time, encountering its slow movement and powerful stability. On this matter of observation and presence Annie Dillard says, "Our life is a faint tracing on the surface of mystery, like the idle curved tunnels of leaf miners on the face of a leaf. We must somehow take a wider view, look at the whole landscape, really see it, and describe what's going on here. Then we can at least wail the right question into the swaddling band of darkness, or, if it comes to that, choir the proper praise."[10]

2. *Practice stillness and silence.* I was talking about the benefits of stillness and silence in a treatment facility, and a man responded, "I can't do that."

"Why not?" I inquired.

"Because my mind is a dangerous neighborhood to walk around in."

I said, "No doubt it is. All of ours are. But you walk around in it all the time already, just with your eyes shut. If you went to a dangerous neighborhood, you wouldn't wear a blindfold, would you?"

To be still requires a deep trust that the world will carry on without us. To be silent is to remember that neither God nor the world especially need our words. Both tell the world that we do not need its distractions or false comforts. And yes, stillness and silence can also cause us to encounter our inner fear, pain, sorrow, and guilt. But as we have already seen, those things do not go away because we ignore them. They still impact us, especially if we try to keep them buried.

Stillness and silence are far more difficult than people think, but also far more important. It can be practiced alone or with a group, and I recommend starting with five minutes. Begin by slowly reading out Psalm 46 or 51 twice over, making sure everyone is in a comfortable position (sitting upright, not slouching, but not tense) and breathing deeply.

Then, be still.

Bodily stillness connects with inner stillness. It helps to have a phrase you repeat in your mind when your thoughts start to run away from you. Many have used the Jesus Prayer for this purpose:

Lord Jesus Christ, Son of God, have mercy on me.

When the five minutes are up, reflect personally or share with one another: Did you struggle staying still? Why? Did you struggle to quiet your thoughts? Where did your mind want to go? Why? Continue practicing on your own and with others, gradually lengthening the amount of time you are still and silent.

Use this as a spur to reflect on your individual and communal attachments to busyness, distraction, and noise. Do you live in an environment in which silence and contemplation are even possible, let alone encouraged? Reflecting on this may require you to radically change the rhythm of your life, particularly if it is currently moving at the pace of the broken world around you. There is a reason many people need to leave chaotic neighborhoods and find a place of peace before they truly begin their healing and restoration from their addictions.

3. *Answer twenty-two questions.* John and Charles Wesley formed the Holy Club at Oxford in 1729. Club members fasted, visited prisoners and the sick, met regularly for devotion and accountability, and came up with a list of twenty-two heart-examining questions to ask of themselves and one another. Check your heart with these questions, daily if possible, and consider meeting weekly with others to go through them one at a time. This is an excellent tool to introduce in a recovery setting as well.

1. Am I consciously or unconsciously creating the impression that I am better than I really am? In other words, am I a hypocrite?
2. Am I honest in all my acts and words, or do I exaggerate?
3. Do I confidentially pass on to another what was told to me in confidence?
4. Can I be trusted?
5. Am I a slave to dress, friends, work, or habits?
6. Am I self-conscious, self-pitying, or self-justifying?
7. Did the Bible live in me today?
8. Do I give it time to speak to me every day?
9. Am I enjoying prayer?
10. When did I last speak to someone else about my faith?
11. Do I pray about the money I spend?
12. Do I get to bed on time and get up on time?
13. Do I disobey God in anything?
14. Do I insist on doing something that makes my conscience uneasy?
15. Am I defeated in any part of my life?
16. Am I jealous, impure, critical, irritable, touchy, or distrustful?

17. How do I spend my spare time?

18. Am I proud?

19. Do I thank God that I am not as other people, especially as the Pharisees who despised the publican?

20. Is there anyone whom I fear, dislike, disown, criticize, hold a resentment toward or disregard? If so, what am I doing about it?

21. Do I grumble or complain constantly?

22. Is Christ real to me?[11]

4. *Encourage daily awareness examen.* This is an ancient Christian practice that translates easily and fruitfully into modern church and recovery settings. It helps us to not let our days run past us unexamined and unremembered. Numerous people in recovery tell me they were finally able to sleep peacefully when following this practice.

a. Set aside intentional time each evening to recall the day you just lived.

b. Reflect on interactions and experiences, thanking God for each moment and confessing any wrongdoing.

c. Ask God to show you how he was present with you.

d. Consider how you felt in the day's experiences and how you feel now as you remember them.

e. Ask God for help for tomorrow.

For They Shall See God

Lest we become overwhelmed with the task of contemplation, hear the good news! The promise to the pure in heart is that they will have a life-giving vision of intimacy with the Creator. This means that once we have courageously encountered the darkness in our hearts, we will find something else there, the "deeper magic" that C. S. Lewis talked about in the Narnia stories. Down in the very deepest parts of our being, underneath our rebellion, fear, and unbelief, we will find the imprint of our Maker in whose image we were created. At the foundation of our hearts is stenciled the words, "Good! Good!"

which God spoke over humanity at our origin. We can proceed into the caverns of our hearts not just with dreadful expectation but also expectant hope.

Karah, whose story began this chapter, took the first steps toward a new purity of heart:

> My father challenged me on my lack of humility. He asked if I thought God was lying when he said he came for the sick, the sinful, and those in need of him. In light of this, I returned again to God. I was beginning to understand that there was no room for him in my life when I was holding on to my motivations of fear of man and fear of rejection. This led to my first submission to the Lord. I resolved to make a full confession of my heart, actions, thoughts, desires, and fears. It was an emptying of sorts, though unfinished. I asked the Lord to reveal to me the areas I had yet to face and committed to dealing with them no matter the time or cost required. This was my first step in letting go of the clutter and impurity in my heart. What followed was an expression of his life, death, and resurrection that changed the way I saw God, myself, and others. For the first time, I glimpsed the world through his eyes, in the image of the love and death of Christ. I experienced and chose to step into the beginning of purity of heart.
>
> This was made gloriously clear and possible through the living Word, the affirmation that the greatest commandment was to love God with everything I had and to love my neighbor as myself. The culmination of this was exhibited through Christ, and I knew that my beginning was in his life, surrendering to love, even unto death.

NINE

Reconciling Community

The Peacemakers

Blessed are the peacemakers, for they will be called children of God.

Matthew 5:9 NIV

Only by restoring the broken connections can we be healed. Connection *is* health.

Wendell Berry, *The Unsettling of America*

Paige was a bright, young Indigenous woman in Vancouver whose tragic life demonstrates the urgent need for peacemaking.[1] A month before her twentieth birthday, Paige died of a drug overdose in the bathroom of a park across the street from my house. Her mother was addicted and could not provide a stable and safe home environment for Paige, and she had been the recipient of professional indifference by governmental services created to protect and support children and youth. She was the subject of thirty child protection reports, moved forty times before her sixteenth birthday, and then moved fifty times to different residences within the DTES between the ages of sixteen and nineteen, including detox facilities, Single Residence Occupancy hotel rooms, shelters, and foster homes. At nineteen her file was closed by the Ministry of Child and Family Development, despite the overwhelming evidence that she was in imminent danger and had been for years. Hers is a story of neglect, abuse, institutional racism, and the shattering societal and personal cost of drug addiction and family breakdown. Her disrupted, sorrowful, peaceless life did not have to be that way. I mourn her appalling, unnecessary death. I also lament that I never got to know my neighbor Paige and heard about her only after she died. Beatitude Communities have the crucial task of incarnating and advocating peace for all the Paiges who are suffering and lost in our dislocated world.

The Ladder

Purity of heart takes us deep into the core of ourselves and roots out hidden falsehood, abuse, idolatry, bitterness, and unbelief so that we might see God in a new way. We do not just rest in that beatific vision, however, because once purified of heart, we are tasked with going back out to make peace in the world. One is tempted to start thinking in superhero terms of righting wrongs and fighting evil, which is why the order of the Beatitudes is so important. There cannot be a hint of self-aggrandizement or glory seeking here. Peacemaking is a sober approach to the violence and fracture in the world, including that which we have caused. True peacemaking is anything but glamorous, but the blessing involved takes us deeper still into union and identification with the Son of God.

Jesus the Peacemaker

If the story of the fall in Genesis 3 describes the effect of humanity's dislocation from creation, from one another, and from God, then Jesus's ministry establishes the basis of peace in all those areas. In every place that humanity has walked away from God, Jesus invites us to come back home and to share in his relationships with God, humanity, and creation. Accepting the invitation to participate in the life of Jesus represents a realignment of our purpose, which was corrupted through sin and pain: "And you, who once were alienated and hostile in mind, doing evil deeds, he has now reconciled in his body of flesh by his death, in order to present you holy and blameless and above reproach before him" (Col. 1:21–22). Jesus is not just our peace with God, but with one another as well. He unites enemies, breaking down "in his flesh the dividing wall of hostility" (Eph. 2:14). Even more, the whole of creation is waiting and groaning for the sons and daughters of God to be revealed so it may be reconciled and set free from its bondage to corruption (Rom. 8:19–23). Who are the sons and daughters of God? Peacemakers, according to this Beatitude.

Irreconcilable Differences

This understanding of peacemaking has direct bearing on addiction and recovery. Broken relationships, guilt over past offenses, and a deep sense of external and internal displacement are at the very heart of addictions. Learning reconciliation is therefore an essential tool for ongoing recovery and full humanity. The spirituality of AA and NA is primarily focused on a reevaluation of our relationship with ourselves, with others, and with God.[2]

A key part of this process is learning to make amends. It takes seven rigorously honest, self-examining steps in AA and NA before this delicate topic is broached. Step 8 is listing all the people we have harmed and becoming willing to make amends, and step 9 is trying to make those amends without causing additional harm. This involves full acknowledgment and ownership of the damage done, combined with practical efforts to redress the wrong and a commitment to not repeat the harm. This lengthy and careful method is far removed from our quick-apology culture, wherein we think a "sorry" suffices for most matters. Amends are not Band-Aids to stop the bleeding; they are the end result of surgery.

Making peace through amends is one of the trickiest parts of the whole journey. Applying scriptural and recovery principles to real-life relationships that have been damaged is very frightening. Some people want to rush straight in before they are ready, and others want to avoid these steps altogether. I have seen it go badly and have had it go badly myself. But at least there is an expectation in recovery that amends *should* be made, and that reconciliation *might* be possible (though amends must be made even where reconciliation does not happen). There is a belief that trying to make peace is not only imaginable but an essential part of health and wholeness. I have rarely seen such commitment to peacemaking in the church. Everyone has stories of unresolved church conflict, ranging from relational breakdowns to congregational splits and denominational breaks. Shouldn't churches have a practice of interpersonal reconciliation at least as rigorous as Alcoholics Anonymous? If reconciliation happens in the church, it is usually ad hoc and mostly due to the inspired efforts of individuals, not because we have developed a culture of peacemaking and amends. Yet making amends follows Paul's instruction to live peaceably with others as far as it is up to us (Rom. 12:18) and Jesus's teaching in Matthew 5:23–24 to be reconciled with our brothers or sisters before leaving our gifts at the altar. If we do not make amends, we carry the unreconciled damage we have done to others in our hearts and minds, and this lack of resolution can easily lead us back down toward the path of addiction. It also leaves those we have harmed in the place of wounding.

War and Peace

Amends-making, however, is not the end of peacemaking. Jesus announces at one point that he brings not peace but a sword and sets family members and households against one another (Matt. 10:34–36). How could this be peacemaking? Peace is not just the absence of conflict; it is the presence of justice, goodness, reconciliation, truth, and right relationship in every sphere. Jesus's peace comes at the cost of losing those things that have led us to false comfort and peace, just as recovery involves relinquishing things, attitudes, and even relationships. Jesus is in the business of true peace, not just surface-level niceties. To be a peacemaker in the model of Jesus, carrying on his ministry of reconciliation, actually brings us into more conflict with the world.

We have endless examples of Christians joining battle to kill their foes, and Christian pacifists or separationists are also well-known.

But Christians who resist the violence of the world, yet still actively and sacrificially engage in the pursuit of justice and the love of enemy, are seen as oddities. The Plowshares Movement is one such oddity. It is a Catholic movement that opposes war and nuclear weapons with loving, insistent nonviolence. They are motivated by Isaiah's prophecy of swords being beaten into plowshares and by the radical idea that union with God includes resisting weapons that are designed to obliterate millions of his children. They believe that the military-industrial economy is based on a societal addiction to violence and greed that thrives on people's fear of the other. So they seek to "disarm" military weaponry, usually through symbolic actions, while retaining the principle of total nonviolence toward people and individual accountability for their actions. This includes submitting to arrests and jail. The movement began with "the Plowshares Eight" in 1980. Eight nonviolent activists, after nine months of prayer, discernment, scriptural meditation, and meticulous planning, trespassed onto a Pennsylvania General Electric plant that manufactured parts for the Minuteman III nuclear missiles. Stunned workers looked on as they beat the missile parts with hammers, poured their blood onto documents and blueprints, and prayed for peace. They were arrested and spent the next ten years arguing their case in court and serving time in prison.[3]

For some this direct action is a step too far, a shocking breach in civility. But peacemaking is not passive; it involves addressing the lack of peace in our world, and doing so will instigate confrontations with worldly powers. Let us not imagine that renouncing our dislocated society and offering Beatitude alternatives will occur without danger, messiness, or pushback. When we call Jesus the Prince of Peace we agree that he is in conflict with the prince of this world and that we are on Jesus's side. The Plowshares Movement takes this very seriously. They seek to accomplish with hammer, blood, and sacrifice what peace talks and apathy often fail to do: prevent actual nuclear weaponry from being built. They refuse to say "'Peace, peace,' when there is no peace" (Jer. 6:14) or to pretend that nuclear proliferation, military domination, and socioeconomic inequality is an acceptable "normal" state for the world. Neither should we accept a dislocated world whose conditions normalize addiction. It is not enough to help individuals; union with Christ involves us in resistance against the systems, structures, and worldviews that keep people alienated and enslaved. And where we find these things continuing to cause alienation and idolatry inside our own communities or hearts, we must ask God to utterly root them out. Peacemakers and children of God must be free to be "repairer[s] of the breach" and "restorer[s] of streets to dwell in" (Isa. 58:12).

PAUSE

Rev. Philip Berrigan wrote this prayer from the Danbury Federal Penitentiary in 1972, while he was serving time for destroying draft records in protest of the Vietnam War: "You are the Prince of Peace, the embodiment of reconciliation. Why is inner peace so elusive to us, community so strange, nonviolence so foreign? Why do we enthrone ourselves; why do we idolize the State? Give us Yourself; give us peace."[4]

What to Do?

1. *Plant a community garden.* Part of the curse in Genesis 3 is a fractured relationship between humanity and creation. We are arguably more dislocated from the earth now than ever, treating the land as an object to be pillaged and consumed and to be viewed primarily in economic and competitive terms, much as we view ourselves and others. Most of us have no idea where our food comes from or how it was produced, by whom, and at what cost. We have no relationship with the soil and often have contempt for or dismiss those who work the soil.

Community gardens are one small way to address this lack of peace. It is remarkably therapeutic for humans to plunge their hands into dirt, to bury seeds, to pull up weeds, to water plants, and to watch fruit, vegetables, and flowers grow. I have been privileged to witness and participate in community gardens around the world and have seen the profound impact of this cultivation of food and beauty on hardened hearts. Gardening is slow, deliberate, and meditative. It reestablishes broken links with soil and never fails to cause conversation among gardeners and curious visitors. It also allows you to see the beginning, middle, and end of a project, and the joy of eating tasty food you have planted and harvested is surprising. We come from the dirt of the earth, and part of peacemaking is learning to care for the land and to use it properly.

2. *Open your home and table to your neighbors.* Eight years ago, Karen stepped out of the normal ministry life and became a peacemaker in her neighborhood. This involved a series of conversions away from adrenaline, deadlines, privacy, control, multitasking, credit-taking, strategic initiatives, and dualistic thinking that separated God-time and her-time. She discovered instead the blessing of slowness, making friends, and waiting on serendipitous encounters with Jesus and with neighbors. Over the past eight years, Karen has opened her home to two hundred and fifty short-term and long-term guests. She got to know her neighbors through visits, attending parties, joining neighborhood activities, and hosting evenings in her home around art, music, movies, and food. Her middle-class neighbors had all experienced the long-term consequences of broken worldviews that had manifested in fractured families, alienation, depression, loneliness, and addiction. One neighbor confessed that she had "never experienced unconditional love—except from my cat." Accompanying this dislocation is a thick layer of distrust and hostility directed toward the church. So Karen does not approach people as the church; she approaches as the neighbor. She cultivates space for conversation, is invited to mediate arguments and hear sorrow, and engages her neighbors in community projects that range from soup nights to sponsoring Syrian refugees. Her desire is to learn with her neighbors what it means to live well in the city and to offer her neighborhood an embodied experience of Jesus's Beatitudes.

This form of peacemaking has little to do with heroism and dramatic moments. It is all about the careful, slow work of presence, hiding oneself in the soil of a place so that good fruit can be borne over time. This is something we can all do if we are prepared to lay down our busyness and need for success. Set aside an evening to host a meal with neighbors. Ask them what they like to eat or suggest a potluck. Turn off the phones to create time and space for real conversation. Hear what is on your neighbors' hearts. Be prepared to accept an invitation given in return. Rather than trying to transform the world, focus on transforming your table so that you can start making peace on your block.

3. *Consider ways you can support vulnerable children and families.* Another friend of mine likes to say, "If you are going to be a peacemaker, you are probably going to have lots of children in your life." She is highlighting the multitude of children around the world, and those in our own communities, who are displaced, orphaned, in difficult home situations, or in a governmental system. Children whose parents or caregivers are emotionally unavailable or entirely absent have been shown to have ongoing difficulty making and sustaining emotional connections.[5] In 2018 the Adverse Childhood Experiences Study found that children who went through multiple traumatic events were 7.4 times more likely to develop alcoholism and 10.3 times more likely to develop an injection drug addiction.[6] Connect this to the reality that three out of every four children in the world experienced interpersonal violence in 2017; that in 2015–16 an estimated seventeen million children were internally displaced and another three hundred thousand applied for asylum; and that children are the most susceptible to exploitative practices, particularly when they are refugees or migrants, and represent 60 percent of trafficking victims in some parts of the world.[7]

Early intervention and support for vulnerable children like Paige and for families in crisis is one of the most important and effective things churches can do to help prevent addiction in the next generation. This can be done by supporting initiatives such as Alongsiders, mentioned in chapter 6, or Brave Global, a campaign that reaches out to girls at risk around the world, affirming them as part of God's answer to the pain and brokenness of the world.[8] Locally there are ways to support vulnerable families as well. It is hugely preferable if possible for families to stay together rather than having children apprehended. Breakfast clubs, after-school activities, parents' groups, and volunteering for respite care are all ways your church can help families and children get the care and support they need.

4. *Look for the lack of peace in your neighborhood and follow the peacemakers.* If you are paying attention, you will come across

issues in your neighborhood that require peacemaking. It may be a hidden opioid crisis, families in need of material support, underfunded schools, refugees trying to find their place in a new community, neighbors who are alienated and lonely, locally owned enterprises threatened by new chain stores, or landlords taking advantage of vulnerable tenants. All of these and more can exacerbate the harm being done in your community.

Jack Gates was a resident of the notorious Balmoral Hotel in Vancouver. The owners were spectacularly failing in their responsibility to their tenants, but people were afraid to lose their homes—or worse—by going public with their complaints. Jack was afraid as well, but he was able to draw on a divine source of courage and hope to become a peacemaker. Four years previous, Jack had been in another hotel, suffering from a drug and alcohol addiction, when, in his words, "Something or someone pulled me off the couch and brought me to my knees. A voice spoke to me saying, 'Thou shalt have no idols before me!'" Then God, as Jack surmised the voice to be, told him that he would be freed from heroin, speed, alcohol, and cigarettes. And he was! No program, no withdrawal, just freedom. Because of this divine intervention, Jack knew he had both the opportunity and the responsibility to stand up to the injustices being visited on the residents of the Balmoral and other such places. He was the first to sign his name to a petition and go public with the conditions they were living in. Jack soon had both his tenancy and his life threatened, but he refused to back down. A coalition of community groups, tenant associations, and pastors gathered around the cause, but Jack and other residents inspired by him were the central actors. Through legal pressure and direct action, the building's ownership is now in the process of being expropriated by the city.

The fight is not over, and not every attempt at peacemaking ends on a happy note. Peacemaking is costly and painful, but we need to discern the lack of peace in our communities and stand with the people of peace we find among our neighbors.

5. *Get educated and involved in truth and reconciliation.* The Truth and Reconciliation Commission in Canada released its final report in 2015 on the history of governmental and church abuse of First Nations communities and made a list of ninety-four specific calls

to action.⁹ Historic abuse and the destruction of kinship communities are major factors in ongoing addictions issues for many people today. The church has significant amends to make, and hopefully a part to play in seeking peace and healing. Inquire to see what truth and reconciliation work is being done in your context and discern how you can get involved.

For They Will Be Called Children of God

To be called a child of God is the greatest gift imaginable, the deepest possible indication of one's union with Jesus Christ, the Son of God. Sons and daughters of God are those who are led by the Spirit of God (Rom. 8:14), who have received God (John 1:12), and who are no longer slaves (Gal. 4:7). The title is not symbolic; it has real-world implications for how to practice righteousness and love our brothers and sisters, not just in words but in actions that meet their needs (1 John 3:10–17). I have frequently been taught about the cost and beauty of this blessing by people living through the most painful and trying of circumstances. The best peacemakers are often those who have known the deepest need for peace in their lives.

My friend Jenn Allen experienced the full measure of the world's injustice and yet emerged a peacemaker. Born into the Tlingit Nation in the Yukon, Jenn was sent to live with relatives in Nova Scotia at the age of three after her mother, a Residential School survivor, went to jail. She did not see her mother again until she was seventeen. By eighteen she was being groomed into the sex trade by older pimps and drug users and spending all her earnings on a drug habit. In Calgary Jenn was charged for defending herself against a police assault, earning her a criminal record that made employment impossible. So she found herself back on the streets, getting drunk and high to numb herself from what she had to do to survive. At twenty-four she was working the streets in Vancouver's DTES, broke, addicted, and living in a brothel. It would be hard to imagine a life less filled with peace.

In her darkest moment Jenn just asked Jesus for a chance. She had little time for religious people, having had negative interactions in the past, but in the DTES she met some Christians who didn't seem to judge her. She began to cautiously open up, though this was not always easy. I remember standing in our kitchen and Jenn being so frustrated with us for not understanding her that she briefly considered stabbing my wife. Jenn persevered, however, and eventually stopped using drugs, left the sex trade, and found safe housing in a recovery home. But she was still dealing with PTSD, panic attacks, and a history that made it hard to get work or be trusted. With a lot of free time on her hands she began volunteering, and then starting her own organizations. Over the next ten years, she founded outreaches to prostituted women that brought them meals while recognizing their dignity and worth, advocacy efforts for federally incarcerated women, programs raising the hopes of imprisoned girls through humanizing activities like make-up and movie nights, and an organization called Cop Watch that holds the Vancouver Police accountable for their interactions with vulnerable people. All the while she was also campaigning for missing and murdered women across Canada. Her life was an exhausting array of activism, and she confesses that she replaced drugs with an addiction to frenetic activity. When she asked God what he really wanted from her, God spoke to her about being grounded and blessed in community. So Jenn committed to a year of discipleship training with us, at the end of which she enrolled as a Salvation Army soldier. Some of her activist friends were annoyed at her involvement with a Christian organization, but she replied, "It's time for First Nations people to become leaders of these organizations." She plans to become a pastor so she can form radical peacemaking communities for those who, like her, have known the terrible absence of peace in their lives.

Jenn is a peacemaker, a blessed child of God. When I asked what that means, she responded, "I know now who I am. I know *whose* I am. I am beloved. And I can act out of that identity of being wanted and loved, not out of what the devil or the world has to say about me."

TEN

Co-suffering Community

The Persecuted

Blessed are those who are persecuted for righteousness' sake, for theirs is the kingdom of heaven. Blessed are you when others revile you and persecute you and utter all kinds of evil against you falsely on my account. Rejoice and be glad, for your reward is great in heaven, for so they persecuted the prophets who were before you.

Matthew 5:10–12

If you evade suffering you also evade the chance of joy. Pleasure you may get, or pleasures, but you will not be fulfilled. You will not know what it is to come home.

Ursula K. Le Guin, *The Dispossessed*

A friend and I prayed together every morning in a community garden on East Hastings, a lively street in the DTES. One morning an altercation began outside the garden fence. A man was collecting a drug debt from another man, and things were getting heated. The debt collector brought out a box of condensed milk cans and began throwing them, one at a time, at the other man, a strange but deadly method of coercion or punishment. We stopped praying and looked at one another, dread on both of our faces. We knew that we could not pray to the God of creation inside the garden and ignore the abuse of his beloved creation outside the garden. Surrender, lament, meekness, righteousness, mercy, purity of heart, and peacemaking all called for a Christlike response. Still, I didn't want to go out there. I am not especially brave, and anyone who is willing to use condensed milk as a weapon is probably not too choosy for targets. But my friend was resolute, so we opened the gate and waded into the conflict, placing ourselves squarely between the two men. The aggressor goggled at us.

"What are you doing?" he asked.

"We are stopping you from hurting him," we replied. The man goggled some more. This did not compute.

"Get out of the way," he ventured.

"No," we said. A small crowd was forming, perhaps eager to see the crazy people get hurt.

The man's anger was building to match his confusion. He had a job to do, and we were preventing him from doing it for no obvious reason. At this point the victim decided to start insulting his attacker. I knew this guy from the neighborhood—he sold drugs in the park where my kids played—and I honestly didn't like him very much. Now I liked him even less and told him to please shut up.

The debt collector, fully enraged, tried a new tactic: "If you don't get out of the way, I will kill you."

I knew this moment would come. Before her martyrdom Ita Ford said, "One who is committed to the poor must risk the same fate as the poor."[1] I didn't want to die, especially for a drug dealer I didn't even like. But we could not allow this kind of violence to go unchecked. If we just ignored the situation, how could we claim affinity with Jesus? I teach men and women in recovery that Jesus is worth laying down your life, giving up your addictions, and facing your fears. I tell them that Jesus is present with them in the struggle. Did I believe it? My fear and unbelief were being fully tested.

"Do what you have to, but we will not let you hurt this man. We won't fight you, but we won't move. This street does not belong to you. It belongs to Jesus." This is what I heard myself say in a shaky voice. I didn't think we were getting out unscathed, yet I can say that Jesus was noticeably close to us in that moment.

My words did not convince. The man called us a few choice names and then grabbed a can and tried to throw it around us. My friend leaped in front of his intended target and took condensed milk to the face for Jesus. Frustrated, the milk-thrower left, shouting out promises of future vengeance.

Both the victim and perpetrator in that story were playing out their broken drama on a block accustomed to violence and drug use, in a city desperate to contain and hide this human misery. The two of us in the garden were dealing with our own attachments and fears. But we knew that Jesus would not just have us be good examples a few feet away, lobbing our message of peace onto the street from behind a chain-link fence. We had to step into the violence, unite ourselves with the fate of the victim, and risk persecution.

The Ladder

Peacemaking sounds nice, but it is the penultimate Beatitude that leads inexorably into the sacrificial depths of persecution. The promise of persecution may seem like an odd place to end a book like this, but it is the final rung of the Beatitude ladder, and there is no getting away from it. When you try to communicate your spiritual awakening to a world still lost in addiction, as step 12 urges people to do, you often find that the world wants nothing to do with it or you. You become a threat to the dysfunctional functioning of the world. The blessings of Jesus do not give us worry-free triumph in this world, but rather the certainty of trouble, which is somehow the blessing to which all the others have been leading.

PAUSE

"When harmed, insulted, or persecuted by someone, do not think of the present but wait for the future, and you will find he has brought you much good, not only in this life but in the life to come."[2]

Outside the Camp with Jesus

Jesus was persecuted for the sake of righteousness, which is a statement worth exploring. He was not persecuted because he was considered a really *good* person or because the religious elite found him to be especially holy. He was considered dangerous precisely because he upended those notions of good and holy. He healed on the wrong days, ate with unclean people, acknowledged and honored foreign and "fallen" women, forgave sin, refused political agendas, judged the temple, touched the outcast, and rebuked the religious and cultural gatekeepers. Worst of all, he claimed that he and the Father were one, which meant that whatever Jesus was doing the Father was supposedly doing as well. Jesus's righteousness looked and smelled different, but it was just a fulfillment of the life God always had in mind for his children. Tamar, Rahab, and Ruth, essential characters in Jesus's genealogy, were all portrayed as righteous for putting their trust in Yahweh, though their actions were considered morally ambiguous. The Hebrew prophets were persecuted for their emphasis on relational righteousness. Jesus was killed for living it. Simone Weil says, "Christ was afflicted. He did not die like a martyr. He died like a common criminal, confused with thieves, only a little more ridiculous."[3]

Jesus's followers are considered blessed for being found worthy to suffer the same fate, because it is the fullest measure of identification we can find with Jesus. Jesus himself says that if the world hated and persecuted him, it will also hate and persecute those who follow him (John 15:18–20). We will not be persecuted for being nice and amenable to the world's cultural norms. We are not being persecuted for *righteousness' sake* when we are despised for cozying up to the world's power brokers, whether conservative or liberal. We are to be different from the patterns of this world, engaged in its suffering but not attached to the systems that create that suffering. We are to be a righteousness conundrum and a scandal to the world.

What is this righteousness that leads to persecution? It is joining with Jesus in his suffering outside the city gates. It means bearing the reproach that he bore outside the camp with the unclean, the undesirables, the orphans, widows, foreigners, sinners, and substance users (Heb. 13:12). Jesus is to be found outside of the clean, safe, comfortable, appropriate places, which means this must be the place where we are found as well. Being outside the city gates in the place of persecution means acknowledging our poverty of spirit and recognizing that we have no claim to be on the inside by dint of our own righteousness. We have come full circle then, poor in spirit and persecuted, and the blessing that Jesus offers to both is identical: theirs is the kingdom of heaven. That the kingdom of heaven can be found outside the places of human power, security, and sanctity is good news to those who live in marginalized spaces.

The beggar at the Beautiful Gate occupied marginal space. He was outside the temple walls, unable to enter because of the uncleanness of his infirmity. Peter and John gave the beggar what they had, the indwelling presence and power of the Spirit, and he was healed to stand and dance inside the temple grounds. But for doing this in Jesus's name the apostles were arrested, tried, imprisoned, threatened, and eventually flogged. After this beating "the apostles left the Sanhedrin, rejoicing because they had been counted worthy of suffering disgrace for the Name" (Acts 5:41 NIV). They were learning what it means to be blessed. Paul explains this blessing in stark terms: "To the present hour we hunger and thirst, we are poorly dressed and buffeted and homeless, and we labor, working with our own hands. When reviled, we bless; when persecuted, we endure; when slandered, we entreat. We have become, and are still, like the scum of the world, the refuse of all things" (1 Cor. 4:11–13).

In his very suffering, Jesus reveals God to be in solidarity with our pain and affliction. Those trapped in addiction can find hope in this embodied presence. Jesus experiences the full alienation and forsakenness of humanity on the cross, and more. It is common to hear people who have been addicted say they have been through hell. Well, whatever hell is, Jesus knows it personally and went further into it than we could ever go. Jesus suffers for us, and with us, that we might rejoice and live with him. But the church needs to carry on this ministry of co-suffering love so that the world's unwanted, isolated, costly, oppressed, and forgotten can still meet Christ in the flesh.

PAUSE

"Christ learned humanhood from his suffering. . . . We learn Christhood from our suffering."[4]

The Isolated

Any journey toward Christ corresponds, therefore, with a journey toward the world's "unwanted," which most definitely includes drug users and alcoholics. If we do not find ourselves in that unwanted category, our addictions and attachments are either more hidden or more societally acceptable, both of which are incredibly dangerous. It also means that we have not effectively resisted the world or associated with those considered undesirable by the world.

Recovery involves facing an enormous amount of temptation and persecution. As people stabilize they often lose touch with their former life, friends, and community. This is normally necessary, at least for a time, because healthy surroundings are a major factor in long-term recovery success. It does, however, lead to guilt and genuine persecution from former associations and isolation as people struggle to find belonging in supportive communities.

My friend Dustin was looking rough. "How are things going?" I asked. He responded, "Things are about to get good." He had just booked into a three-month treatment center outside of the city and was waiting for his ride. I looked around at the drugs being dealt and used on the street around us and offered to wait with him. Over the next half hour, four different people asked how he was doing. When Dustin told them that he was going to treatment, they each congratulated him and then offered to buy him one last hit. Each time Dustin looked at me, turned back to the person offering him free heroin, and said, "No thank you." I had never seen such blatant temptation at such a vulnerable time. I believe they were trying to be generous, but I also believe the Enemy of our souls was attempting to sabotage Dustin's entry into recovery and new life. I thought of 1 Peter 5:8–9: "Be sober-minded; be watchful. Your adversary the devil prowls around like a roaring lion, seeking someone to devour. Resist him, firm in your faith, knowing that the same kinds of suffering are being experienced by your brotherhood throughout the world." Dustin later told me he would not have been able to resist the temptation alone.

My friend Rusty has been in and out of treatment for years, resulting from a childhood in foster care where he never felt that he fit in. He recently had a powerful encounter with Jesus, was filled with the Holy Spirit, and gained an entirely new perspective on his created purpose and on how recovery can help him live it out. He longs to share his hope in Jesus with the people around him. The other guys in his recovery program, however, are less enthusiastic and have begun isolating Rusty. This can happen in twelve-step circles when someone assigns a name and concrete identity to his or her Higher Power. People inside and outside of recovery prefer it when the God of your understanding is vague enough to include any meaning but soft enough to preclude any ethical requirements. Rusty's newfound faith is a barrier to fellowship with certain of his peers, but his old-found addiction makes him feel unwelcome in most church settings. He is in a recovery no-man's-land.

It takes enormous resolve and grace to handle temptation and isolation. People in recovery are trying to do this while dealing with old emotional issues and learning a new way of life without the old ways of coping. They often find themselves misunderstood and in conflict with the messages of the world around them, distrusted in their former relationships, and held under suspicion in new relationships. Beatitude Communities need to understand and embrace the role of offering kinship community to the isolated in a hostile world.

PAUSE

"I want a small monastery, like the house of a poor workman who is not sure if he will find work and bread, who with all his being shares the suffering of the world."[5]

The Costly

We must not romanticize persecution. We do not seek persecution for its own sake but should expect it as we join in ever-closer union with Jesus and the despised of the world. Some people are so despised that ministering to them carries a huge cost, and it is difficult to imagine what community with them could look like.

I have friends in this situation, and they are costly. One man, because of the horrific nature of his crimes, is restricted in his contact with most people, particularly children. He is as isolated and despised a person as I know, and that is saying something. His parole officer once asked me, with his client present, "Do you really think this guy is worth your time?" Working with him is costly because most other people—even in jail and recovery programs—hate and suspect him, which extends to me when I am seen visiting with him. The fact that he was viciously abused as a child, which contributed to his own brokenness and abusive behavior as an adult, does little to mitigate the hatred. Pastoring him risks being painted with the same brush, being isolated and distrusted by everyone from ex-cons to social workers to police officers. He claims to love Jesus, and I know that Jesus loves him, but he is still a threat and can never be welcomed to my home, my table, my family. Is he worth it?

Beatitude Community means encountering and accompanying one another in the darkest places of our struggles. One woman in our community has maintained decade-long relationships with at-risk youth she met through school outreach. She has walked with them through family breakdowns, drug and alcohol use, deaths, the start of new families, rejection, and through her own emotional and spiritual struggles as well. These children, now adults, may never attend a church, but they have been encountered again and again by Jesus through this woman's costly love and perseverance. Have they been worth it?

My wife, Cherie, and other women in our community spent days and nights outside a friend's apartment because they knew she needed a supportive presence the moment she emerged. When she finally came outside, they walked and prayed with her until she threw away her crack pipe and was ready to go to a safe place. That sounds like a victory, and it was in the moment, but the situation has repeated several times since, and each time it becomes more difficult for people to sacrifice their time and energy. James tells us to "count it all joy" when we face "trials of various kinds, for you know that the testing of your faith produces steadfastness" (James 1:2–3). But trials are *hard*. Persevering is *hard*. People are often ungrateful, rude, or demanding. Sometimes those you have tried to help become your most vocal critics, claiming you never did anything for them and that your so-called love is a big lie, just a way of feeling good about yourself or a scam to get money or attention. That really hurts, especially when you wonder if it is at least partly true. Yet we are still called to love, because it is not up to us to decide how people respond. Blessed are you when people "utter all kinds of evil against you falsely on my account" (Matt. 5:11). Once again, it doesn't *feel* very blessed. Is it worth it?

In these scenarios and more, we have been advised to give people up as lost causes and to consider the damage that would be done to our ministry if we kept pursuing them. And in some of these cases our ministry *was* damaged, and people got hurt or burned out. Other times we gave up on people too quickly out of fear, frustration, or just failure. We have not yet figured out the balance between persevering in love and acknowledging that we cannot be anyone's savior, and I'm not sure we ever will.

Of course, there are costlier forms of persecution that Jesus followers endure around the world, and we can learn much about the nature of persevering love from them. Nina met Jesus in the Soviet Union in the 1980s and began outreach work among addicted youth and people with HIV/AIDS. In 2000 she began working with Chechen refugee children in Grozny who had escaped the war. She loved the work but had to deal with threats directed against the project and against her personally. In 2002, the day she opened her second community center for Chechen children, Nina was kidnapped by Chechen bandits. She was chained up in dark, dank, mice- and snake-infested pits for five and a half months while her captors tried to get a ransom for her. She was sometimes left alone for up to a week with little food or water, in rain and subzero temperatures. To keep her mind occupied she prayed, composed poems, and wrote notes of thanks to her captors for the food, medicine, and occasional encouragement they gave her. She was regularly moved by God to pray for her captors. Her love for them, she asserts, came from Jesus's teaching: "But I say to you, Love your enemies and pray for those who persecute you, so that you may be sons of your Father who is in heaven. For he makes his sun rise on the evil and on the good, and sends rain on the just and on the unjust" (Matt. 5:44–45). When she was finally released, officials wanted her to go to Saint Petersburg, thinking it was too dangerous for her to work anymore among the Chechens. She went to Saint Petersburg, for two weeks. Then she returned to Grozny to spend another year with Chechen refugees and open a third children's center. Nina says, "I bear no malice or offense against the Chechens. I don't think I should give myself credit for this. It is the way God worked in my heart."

Lord, if we can bear the cost, please work in our hearts like this.

PAUSE

"The poor tell us who we are. The prophets tell us who we can be. So we hide the poor and kill the prophets."[6]

The Oppressed

James Cone writes, "When one resists evil, suffering is an inevitable consequence of that resistance."[7] Sometimes accompanying people and acknowledging their dignity involves standing with them against persecution and oppression. We received a phone call early one morning telling us that police were ticketing homeless people and confiscating their possessions in Oppenheimer Park. We rushed down and confronted the officers, who were obeying city orders to clean up the neighborhood in advance of the 2010 Olympics. It is technically a bylaw infraction to be in a public park overnight and to erect a tent or other structure to sleep in. But the police and city were more hesitant to harass non-homeless, non-vulnerable people, so park residents and neighbors began the Oppenheimer Park Peace Camp. A corner of the park was set aside for a round-the-clock camp of homeless and housed people resisting Vancouver's efforts to sweep the poor under the rug. The camp was hosted by park residents who helped keep it drug and alcohol free. It became a place of community, songs, laughter, prayer, and hanging out on the couches that people placed there. I participated one night in a giant prayer circle of people from every conceivable background. I don't know that I have ever seen a more genuine example of church. Later, some of us slept without tents in the pouring rain on the front lawn of City Hall in order to display the ridiculousness of the city bylaw. The ticketing of the homeless in Oppenheimer Park ceased for a time.

The persecution we received for these actions from the official agents of the city was minimal, and we must remember that it is the homeless, the poor, the addicted, and the vulnerable who normally face the brunt of the world's ignorance, hatred, and fear. The difficulties we faced for these efforts came mainly from *inside* the church. Our attempts to join cause with the vulnerable threatened certain relationships with corporate and government funders. I was nearly fired for bringing homeless and addicted friends into my house and was told in one meeting that "it would be no shame" if we just left. This kind of persecution, less sharp than what my friends face daily but still painful, first made me angry and then incredibly sad. I freely confess that we have made many mistakes and failed repeatedly to communicate truth in love. Where we are wrong, we should long to be put right, and even where we are in the right, we should let love and humility guide our every action. But it still felt like every attempt to get closer to the righteous heart of Jesus caused some in the church to further distance themselves from us. We began to experience a small amount of the isolation and rejection felt by the poor all over the world and throughout history. It hurts, a lot. But if remaining true to Jesus means being misunderstood, miscategorized, rejected, and wounded, even by people we love, then this is a cost we must accept. Even more, we must learn to bless those who persecute us, and not to curse them (Rom. 12:14). Others have lived this out to a much greater degree than we have. I think of my First Nations friends who experienced systemic racism and abuse from the church growing up but still love Jesus and serve the body of Christ. Many face suspicion from their own families and communities for their faith, while still encountering racism and ignorance from within the church. I am staggered by their perseverance and by the depth and power of their hope and trust in Jesus. Another friend of mine says that in his attempts to follow Jesus, particularly in the areas of peacemaking and standing with the vulnerable, he has known nothing but trouble from both the world and the church. He and his community are routinely ignored, rejected, slandered, and in one season regularly imprisoned for their peacemaking witness. Incredibly, they still hold onto hope for the church, which is a testament to the work of blessing that Jesus has done in their hearts.

PAUSE

"So we do not lose heart. Though our outer self is wasting away, our inner self is being renewed day by day. For this light momentary affliction is preparing for us an eternal weight of glory beyond all comparison, as we look not to the things that are seen but to the things that are unseen. For the things that are seen are transient, but the things that are unseen are eternal." (2 Cor. 4:16–18)

The Forgotten

I do not wish to imply that I or our community have lived out this last Beatitude faithfully or successfully. I am as averse to persecution as anyone and have made decisions that minimize the cost of relationship to myself far too frequently. I am still working on my attachments to comfort, control, being liked, and being "right." I often react with defensiveness and hurt when facing opposition, which can lead to self-pity, obsessive thinking, and harmful behaviors. These attachments have kept me from fully accessing the blessing of the persecuted, and have proven costly to my friends, my family, and my community.

Lord, have mercy.

One of the ways God has challenged my selfish attachments is by reminding me of the *forgotten*: those whose physical, mental, and/

or emotional suffering seems to have gone beyond the reasonable help of detox and recovery. Confronted with these forgotten, I am forced to face the question: Is Jesus still present for those who are so far outside the camp that they may never be liberated in this world from pain, fear, and addiction?

Leena has been living with catastrophic physical and mental illness for years and may be the most marginalized woman in the DTES, the least welcome in most places, the embodiment of pain and rejection. Despite this she has played a significant role in our community, serving as a maid of honor at weddings, a godmother to children, the life of many parties, and the distributor of ferocious hugs on street corners. I haven't seen Leena in a long while, however. She is easy to lose track of and even forget about, one of the many who go out of mind when they go out of sight. But not by all. I know Leena is still alive because my friend Caitlyn works in her supportive housing and visits her. Caitlyn does a beautiful job reminding people that Leena exists. She gently but correctly rebuked me for not visiting and shares pictures of Leena from weddings and community events so people can see what her life was like before she lost her mobility and communication.

I was blessed recently to visit Leena, who is now confined to a wheelchair and can "speak" only in grunts. She is given strong drugs each day to ease her incredible suffering, and everyone expects she will die soon, though many predicted that she would die a long time ago. She is a miracle of perseverance. Still, Leena needs constant assistance from support staff, street nurses, and a friend who stays faithfully by her side day and night. This friend told me of their hellish journey through Leena's bone infections, hospitalizations, and near-death experiences until they arrived at the simple and safe apartment they are now in, which has a stunning view of the North Shore mountains. I marveled at his loving and costly commitment to Leena. I further marveled that Leena remembered me and many of the people from our community whose lives she had touched.

What does recovery or Beatitude Community look like for Leena? I believe in healing and hope and will continue visiting her and praying for a miracle. But "success" cannot just mean that she gets better and is able to approximate a normal life. There is no conceivable point now where she will be well enough to undergo detox and recovery. To be associated with her is to be forcefully reminded of the failure of society, the failure of the health-care system, the failure of family, the failure of the church, the failure of community, and my own personal failure to love her well. To commit to Leena is to acknowledge that her life is not about what I think is possible, or even good, for her. It is to join her in being ignored and forgotten. And it is to trust that Jesus joins her there as well.

I have a lot to learn before I can say I genuinely understand or embrace this, and I confess to being daunted at the thought of what truly committing to Leena looks like. I cannot "save" her or "fix" her. I can do better at remembering her, though, and I will try, because I remember the blessing she offered us.

Our community was going through a painful and confusing season. We were asking one another if our neighborhood friends were genuinely welcome in the heart of our fellowship, or if we just liked the idea of "doing life" with the poor but preferred less costly relationships. In other words, were we hypocrites, white-washed tombs? Not quite knowing what else to do, we prepared to pray together in silence one evening and contemplate the following questions: Do we hear the voice of the Lord through the cries of the oppressed and broken in our midst? Are they central to us?

At the very moment we bowed our heads, a loud, clamorous cry erupted from the bottom of the staircase. It was Leena, newly released from jail, who had decided to attend our gathering. As she proceeded riotously up the stairs, we knew there would be no silent prayer, as even at this point she could not control her flailing limbs or the volume of her speech. She finally crashed into our meeting, looked around, and asked what we were doing. Ignoring my response, she proceeded to visit each person in turn, lift them up, give them a hug and a kiss, and yell, "I love you!" directly into their face. Ten full minutes later she finished by sitting down in the very center of our circle. The Lord had heard our prayer.

Though some of our community members befriended her well through the years, I don't believe we were able to love Leena to the extent that she needed. Maybe we just didn't know how, or maybe we were afraid of the cost. Her jarring presence in our lives was a distinct challenge to our claims to love the poor, and the relationship we have had with her represents more grace on her part than ours. That night, as she came to us with her brokenness, her insistence, and her love, she spoke the words of God over us. Leena revealed that God offers his immediate presence, shorn of pretense, because he offered it to us through her. Through Leena we met Jesus outside the camp, and he hugged us and told us that he loves us. In the presence of Leena we gained something of the kingdom of heaven. Understanding this adds a whole new element to the consequences of forgetting her.

Lord, have mercy.

What to Do?

1. *Find the unwanted, the isolated, the costly, the persecuted, and the forgotten outside the camp in your neighborhood.* We come back to reading your neighborhood, trying to hear its heart, its pain, and its hope. Ask God to show you those who are outside the camp all around you and make a commitment as a community to join them there. Seek out those who have been abandoned, rejected, and considered nothing, and look for the signs of Christ in their midst. If you are discomforted by this suggestion and want to respond that God also loves the insiders and the rich, then I agree. But remember that the starting point of both faith and recovery is poverty of spirit. If insiders want to commune with Jesus, we must humble ourselves and come outside the camp as well. This is not a barrier to the kingdom of heaven; it is just the way Jesus has shown us. Jesus welcomes everyone into his house, but the journey begins and ends outside the camp.

2. *Practice Jesus's Beatitudes within a community of co-suffering love.* For the church to be a genuine community of co-suffering love that can stand against the darkness, the chaos, and the void, we need the experience of those who know what it means to persevere through pain and persecution. One man I know says, "Us addicts are used to feeling very foolish, very low-standing, very much *under* the world. But we know that God loves us even in that place." What if we could really learn and practice this? Most people in recovery are experienced at helping one another in the face of serious temptation and trial:

the final three steps of the twelve steps are all about maintenance, perseverance, and sharing good news with others. Reading and practicing the Beatitudes together from below with the "foolish," "weak," and "low and despised in the world" helps us gain new perspectives and challenges our attachments to the things that seem "wise" and "strong" (1 Cor. 1:27–29).

For Theirs Is the Kingdom of Heaven

When we say "kingdom of heaven," people think of judgment day. This is not inappropriate, as Jesus talks about the last things and he *is* a judge (Matt. 25:31–46). The dislocation, idolatry, fear, enslavement, and addiction of the world—including that of the church— will fall under Christ's final, righteous judgment. Whatever trust we put in anything other than Christ will be dismayed as the kingdom of heaven decisively overturns the systems, structures, and sin that have long kept humanity in bondage. Death itself will die (1 Cor. 15:24–26). To whom then belongs the kingdom of heaven, promised at the beginning and the end of the Beatitudes? It belongs to Christ. Yet he gifts it to those who have been drawn upward by love into his divine life, who have climbed the ladder of the Beatitudes, starting with poverty of spirit and arriving at persecution for Jesus's sake. The kingdom of heaven is not so much a place as it is a dynamic identification with the ongoing joy and suffering of Christ in the world. Simone Weil wrote, "Love is a direction and not a state of the soul. If one is unaware of this, one falls into despair at the first onslaught of affliction."[8] We are moving either in the direction of addiction and alienation or in the direction of connection with God and community. Relationship is heaven's answer to the dislocation of addiction, both now and forever.

This focus on relationship cannot be overstressed at the end of our exploration of addiction and Beatitude Community, because Jesus's description of the blessed life is not simply a set of steps to follow. The Beatitudes are not a self-help guide to moral betterment or a magic formula for success in life or in recovery. They are far more exciting and frightening than that. Jesus invites us into his story, which is also an invitation into the story of full humanity, and the final story of creation's redemption. This is the story of co-suffering love: for God so loved the world—the world that rejected God, hated God, replaced God, arranged itself without God—that he sent Jesus to bear and overcome the world's flesh, suffering, sin, and even death. Then Jesus sent his people, the ones carrying his name and his Spirit, into the world to embody his message in Beatitude Communities. Jesus promised that not even the worst of our trials could tear apart the union he created: "I am with you always, to the end of the age" (Matt. 28:20). Paul, accustomed to persecution, affirms this: "For I am sure that neither death nor life, nor angels nor rulers, nor things present nor things to come, nor powers, nor height nor depth, nor anything else in all creation, will be able to separate us from the love of God in Christ Jesus our Lord" (Rom. 8:38–39).

This book began by affirming hope in the face of addiction's devastations. That hope shines throughout the Beatitudes as Jesus confronts the pain, sin, and dislocation common to humanity with the promise of blessing. The blessing offered to drug users, alcoholics, those with socially acceptable attachments, and everyone else is the possibility of an eternally deepening union with Christ. This is the purpose of the Beatitudes: not to bring us sobriety, progressive politics, good morals, or full churches, but to guide us toward the recovery of Jesus's divine image in us and in one another. If we seek this first, everything else that we need will come too. This divine union is not theoretical; it is actual, effective, and designed to be experienced as a reality for our present bodies, souls, and spirits. By this union we may taste the firstfruits of heaven's liberation and comfort now, individually, and especially in kinship relationships with others. But we must confess that we do not yet have the fullness of it. In this life we will still know sorrow and struggle, fear and death, and the ever-present lure of attachment and addiction. But we are not left alone, without blessing or without hope.

Hope is the currency of Beatitude Communities.

Friends, there is hope.

Resources

Here is a brief list of sources if you are looking for immediate help in the area of addictions and recovery:

Addiction and Grace: Love and Spirituality in the Healing of Addiction, by Gerald G. May. In this classic text of faith and psychology, May offers remarkable insight on the environmental, spiritual, emotional, and physical realties of addiction and the place of faith and grace in recovery.

Recovery: Freedom from Our Addictions, by Russell Brand. Brand is best known as a comedian, but he has written a beautiful book drawing from his experiences as an addict. It is very raw and raucous, and perhaps not for everyone, but it certainly speaks the language of addiction and recovery in a way that is accessible to people who are hurting.

In the Realm of Hungry Ghosts: Close Encounters with Addiction, by Gabor Maté. A seminal work that presents addiction as the result of unprocessed pain.

"Healing Addiction through Community: A Much Longer Road Than It Seems?" by Bruce K. Alexander, http://www.brucek alexander.com/articles-speeches/healing-addiction-through -community-a-much-longer-road-than-it-seems2. Alexander proposes the Dislocation Theory of Addiction, which suggests that it is not a failing of morality but a failing of community that leads most of us into addictions and attachments.

The Big Book of Alcoholics Anonymous: Including Twelve Steps, Guides and Prayers, by Bill Wilson and Aaron Cohen. Essential reading for anyone wanting to be involved in recovery communities.

Celebrate Recovery. A Christ-centered twelve-step recovery program being used around the world: https://www.celebraterecovery.com.

Freedom Session. A twenty-week, intense healing and discipleship program for people with all kinds of addictions, attachments, hurts, and hang-ups: https://freedomsession.com.

"The Creative Way Down," an Infinitum resource by Aaron White and Danielle Strickland. This is a three-month practical discipleship resource for churches and groups, based on the Beatitudes and including reflections on twelve-step recovery: https://infinitumlife.com/creative-way-down.

Notes

Introduction

1. Richard Rohr, *Breathing under Water: Spirituality and the Twelve Steps* (Cincinnati: St. Anthony Messenger, 2011), 115.

Chapter 1 Broken

1. Frederick Buechner, *The Sacred Journey: A Memoir of Early Days* (San Francisco: Harper & Row, 1982), 46.

2. Richard Rohr, *Breathing under Water: Spirituality and the Twelve Steps* (Cincinnati: St. Anthony Messenger, 2011), 65.

3. Gerald G. May, *Addiction and Grace: Love and Spirituality in the Healing of Addictions* (San Francisco: HarperSanFrancisco, 2007), 14.

4. Travis Lupick, "Vancouver City Council Told Fentanyl Meant 2017 Saw a Record Number of Drug-Overdose Deaths," *Georgia Straight*, January 17, 2018, https://www.straight.com/news/1020446/vancouver-city-council-told-fentanyl-meant-2017-saw-record-number-drug-overdose-deaths.

5. Caryn Pearson, Teresa Janz, and Jennifer Ali, "Mental and Substance Use Disorders in Canada," Statistics Canada, last modified November 27, 2015, http://www.statcan.gc.ca/pub/82-624-x/2013001/article/11855-eng.htm.

6. "Statistics on Addiction in America," Addiction Center, July 15, 2019, https://www.addictioncenter.com/addiction/addiction-statistics.

7. "Addiction: Our Stupid Friend," *Float House* (blog), 2015, https://floathouse.ca/blog-archive/addiction-our-stupid-friend?.

8. Bruce K. Alexander, "Addiction: Hopeful Prophecy from a Time of Despair," *Bruce K. Alexander* (blog), September 9, 2017, http://www.brucekalexander.com/articles-speeches/dislocation-theory-addiction/290-addiction-a-hopeful-prophecy-from-a-time-of-despair-2.

9. Brené Brown, "Everyone Has a Story," *Brené Brown* (blog), June 7, 2018, https://brenebrown.com/blog/2018/06/07/everyone-has-a-story.

10. Alexander, "Addiction."

11. Alexander, "Addiction."

12. Alexander, "Addiction."

13. Alexander, "Addiction."

14. Wendell Berry, *The Unsettling of America: Culture and Agriculture* (San Francisco: Sierra Club Books, 1977), 4.

15. Timothy Keller, *Walking with God through Pain and Suffering* (New York: Dutton, 2013), 14.

16. Alexander, "Addiction." The language of being *cured* is contentious. AA and NA programs maintain that an addict is always an addict, and they must always be alert and aware of their temptations. Their hope for ongoing sobriety is the continued work of the program. But there *is* hope that this life can be maintained, which suggests a marked difference between this approach and one that denies the importance, or even the possibility, of a drug-and-alcohol-free life.

17. Alexander, "Addiction."

18. Charles Taylor, *Sources of the Self: The Making of the Modern Identity* (Cambridge, MA: Harvard University Press, 1989), 510.

19. Keller, *Walking with God*, 74.

20. Chris Stapleton and Lee Thomas Miller, "Whiskey and You," Track 5 on Chris Stapleton, *Traveller*, Mercury Nashville, 2015.

21. Ed Yong, "A Landmark Study on the Origins of Alcoholism, *The Atlantic*, June 21, 2018, https://www.theatlantic.com/science/archive/2018/06/a-landmark-study -in-the-origins-of-alcoholism/563372. This study determined that an imbalance in a brain chemical (GABA) in certain rats could inhibit their ability to deal with fear and stress, thus increasing their likelihood of becoming addicted. The same chemical imbalance is found in humans who are addicted, supporting the idea that unprocessed fear and stress is a major fact in addiction.

22. Don Pinnock, *Gang Town* (Cape Town, South Africa: Tafelberg, 2016), 205.

23. May, *Addiction and Grace*, 14.

24. Rohr, *Breathing under Water*, xxiii.

25. Russell Brand, *Recovery: Freedom from Our Addictions* (London: Bluebird, 2017), 66.

26. Brand, *Recovery*, 96.

27. Brand, *Recovery*, 62.

28. Alexander, "Addiction."

29. Travis Lupick, *Fighting for Space: How a Group of Drug Users Transformed One City's Struggle with Addiction* (Vancouver: Arsenal Pulp, 2017), 16.

30. Lupick, *Fighting for Space*, 17.

31. Simon Little, "Hallucinogen That Heals? One B.C. Psychotherapist's Experience with Ayahuasca," *Global News*, April 25, 2018, https://globalnews.ca/news/4166406/aya huasca-mental-health-addiction.

32. Gregory Boyle, *Barking to the Choir: The Power of Radical Kinship* (New York: Simon & Schuster, 2017), 56.

33. Gabor Maté, *In the Realm of Hungry Ghosts: Close Encounters with Addiction* (Toronto: Vintage Canada, 2012).

34. Viet Thanh Nguyen, ed., *The Displaced: Refugee Writers on Refugee Lives* (New York: Abrams, 2018), 15.

35. Glenn Smith, "Reading Your Community: Towards an Authentic Encounter with the City," http://direction.ca/wp-content/uploads/2018/04/Reading-your-community.pdf.

36. The 100 block of East Hastings is at the very heart of the DTES community.

37. A wealthier, more comfortable neighborhood about a twenty-minute drive from the DTES.

38. Bud Osborn, *Hundred Block Rock* (Vancouver: Arsenal Pulp, 1999), 79–80. Used by permission.

Chapter 2 Blessed

1. Laurel Dykstra, *Set Them Free: The Other Side of Exodus* (Maryknoll, NY: Orbis, 2002), 198.

2. Jim Forest, "Climbing the Ladder of the Beatitudes," *Jim and Nancy Forest* (blog), August 16, 2017, http://jimandnancyforest.com/2017/08/climbing-the-ladder-of-the-beatitudes.

3. Forest, "Climbing the Ladder."

4. Ron Dart, "The Beatitudes (Matthew 5:3–12)—Translation by Ron Dart," *Clarion Journal of Spirituality and Justice*, February 5, 2018, http://www.clarion-journal.com/clarion_journal_of_spirit/2018/02/the-beatitudes-matthew-53-12-translation-by-ron-dart.html.

5. Stephen Finlan and Vladimir Kharlamov, eds., *Theosis: Deification in Christian Theology* (Eugene, OR: Pickwick, 2006), 1.

6. Athanasius, *On the Incarnation*, trans. John Behr (Yonkers, NY: St. Vladimir's Seminary Press, 2011), 38.

7. Symeon the New Theologian, quoted in Alister E. McGrath, *Christian Theology: An Introduction* (Oxford: Oxford University Press, 1997), 353.

8. Charles R. Wilson, "Christology: The Incarnate Word of God," in *A Contemporary Wesleyan Theology: Biblical, Systematic, and Practical*, vol. 1, ed. Charles W. Carter (Grand Rapids: Asbury Press, 1983), 350.

9. John Milbank, "Beauty and the Soul," in John Milbank, Graham Ward, and Edith Wyschogrod, *Theological Perspectives on God and Beauty* (Harrisburg, PA: Trinity Press International, 2003), 8.

10. Kenneth Tanner, "Our Ascension with Christ—Cooperating with Christ in the Renewal of All Things," *Clarion Journal of Spirituality and Justice*, June 7, 2018, http://www.clarion-journal.com/clarion_journal_of_spirit/ 2018/06/our-ascension-with-christ-cooperating-with-christ-in-the-renewal-of-all-things-kenneth-tanner.html.

11. Athanasius, *Incarnation*, 38.

12. Tanner, "Our Ascension with Christ."

13. Liviu Petcu, "The Doctrine of Epektasis. One of the Major Contributions of Saint Gregory of Nyssa to the History of Thinking," *Revista Portuguesa de Filosofia* 73, no. 2 (2017): 771.

14. Simone Weil, *Waiting for God* (New York: Perennial, 2001), xxxii.

15. Bob Ekblad, *The Beautiful Gate: Enter Jesus' Global Liberation Movement* (Burlington, WA: People's Seminary, 2017), 70.

16. Christopher C. H. Cook, "Spirituality and Alcohol Dependence," in *Identification and Treatment of Alcohol Dependency*, ed. Colin R. Martin (Keswick, UK: M&K Update, 2008), 295.

17. Gregory of Nyssa, *The Life of Moses*, trans. Abraham J. Malherbe and Everett Ferguson, Classics of Western Spirituality (Mahwah, NJ: Paulist Press, 1978), 115.

18. Dallas Willard, *The Divine Conspiracy: Rediscovering Our Hidden Life in God* (San Francisco: HarperSanFrancisco, 1998), 408.

19. Rebekah Eklund, "Blessed Are the Image-Bearers: Gregory of Nyssa and the Beatitudes," *Anglican Theological Review* 99, no. 4 (Fall 2017): 730–31.

20. Dorothy Day, *The Long Loneliness* (San Francisco: HarperSanFrancisco, 1981), 286.

21. "About Us," San Patrignano, https://www.sanpatrignano.com/about-us.

22. Gregory Boyle, *Barking to the Choir: The Power of Radical Kinship* (New York: Simon & Schuster, 2017), 7.

23. Bruce K. Alexander, "Healing Addiction through Community: A Much Longer Road Than It Seems?" *Bruce K. Alexander* (blog), May 14, 2015, http://www.bruce alexander.com/articles-speeches/healing-addiction-through-community-a-much-longer -road-than-it-seems2.

24. Personal conversation with Rob and Amy Reardon, Seattle, Washington, October 2018.

25. Jacqueline Pullinger, "Drug Rehabilitation: Transformation through a Reparenting Approach," International Conference on Tackling Drug Abuse, March 5, 2018, https://www .nd.gov.hk/en/conference_proceedings/ Drugs_proBK_Part4/Drugs_proBK_JacqP.pdf.

26. Gregory of Nyssa, *The Lord's Prayer/The Beatitudes*, trans. Hilda Graef, Ancient Christian Writers 18 (Westminster, MD: Newman, 1954), 24–25.

Chapter 3 Surrendered Community

1. Isaac the Syrian, "Homily 8," in *The Ascetical Homilies of Saint Isaac the Syrian*, 2nd ed. (Boston: Holy Transfiguration Monastery, 2011), http://www.htmp.org/St-Isaac -Ascetical-Homilies/overview.html, 185–88.

2. "The Twelve Steps of Alcoholics Anonymous," Alcoholics Anonymous, https:// www.aa.org/assets/en_US/smf-121_en.pdf.

3. *Alcoholics Anonymous: The Story of How Many Thousands of Men and Women Have Recovered from Alcoholism*, 4th ed. (New York: Alcoholics Anonymous World Services, 2001), 59.

4. Timothy Keller, *Walking with God through Pain and Suffering* (New York: Dutton, 2013), 50.

5. Elder Ephraim, *Counsels from the Holy Mountain: Selected from the Letters and Homilies of Elder Ephraim* (Florence, AZ: St. Anthony's Greek Orthodox Monastery, 1999), 102.

6. Martin Luther, quoted in Keller, *Walking with God*, 50.

7. Saint Macarius the Great, quoted in Matthew the Poor, *Orthodox Prayer Life: The Interior Way* (New York: St. Vladimir's Seminary Press, 2003), 183.

8. Catherine of Genoa, "Life and Teachings," in *Devotional Classics*, ed. Richard Foster and James Bryan Smith (San Francisco: HarperSanFrancisco, 1990), 213.

9. C. S. Lewis, *Mere Christianity* (New York: Macmillan, 1977), 189–90.

10. Dorothy Day, *The Long Loneliness* (San Francisco: HarperSanFrancisco, 1981), 81.

11. *House*, season 3, episode 11, "Words and Deeds," directed by Daniel Sackheim, written by Leonard Dick, aired January 9, 2007, on Fox, https://www.nbc.com/house /episodes/season-3.

12. Keller, *Walking with God*, 53.

13. Viktor E. Frankl, *Psychotherapy and Existentialism: Selected Papers on Logotherapy* (New York: Pocket Books, 1967), 122.

14. Jean Vanier, *Be Not Afraid* (Toronto: Griffin House, 1975), ix.

15. Vanier, *Be Not Afraid*, 21.

16. Gerald G. May, *Addiction and Grace: Love and Spirituality in the Healing of Addictions* (San Francisco: HarperSanFrancisco, 2007), 17.

17. Jean Vanier, *From Brokenness to Community* (Mahwah, NJ: Paulist Press, 1992), 20.

18. Oscar Romero, *The Violence of Love* (Maryknoll, NY: Orbis, 2004), 40.

Chapter 4 Lamenting Community

1. Timothy Keller, *Walking with God through Pain and Suffering* (New York: Dutton, 2013), 49.

2. Meghan O'Rourke, "Good Grief: Is There a Better Way to Be Bereaved?" *New Yorker*, February 1, 2010, https://www.newyorker.com/magazine/2010/02/01/good-grief.

3. Leymah Gbowee and Carol Mithers, *Mighty Be Our Powers: How Sisterhood, Prayer, and Sex Changed a Nation at War* (New York: Beast Books, 2011), 106–7.

4. Cornel West and Christa Buschendorf, *Black Prophetic Fire* (Boston: Beacon, 2014), 162.

5. Saint John Climacus, quoted in Matthew the Poor, *Orthodox Prayer Life: The Interior Way* (New York: St. Vladimir's Seminary Press, 2003), 227.

6. Gail R. O'Day, "Surprised by Faith: Jesus and the Canaanite Woman," in *A Feminist Companion to Matthew*, ed. Amy-Jill Levine (Sheffield: Sheffield Academic Press, 2001), 120–21.

7. Brian Heasley, ed., *Writing on the Wall: Prayers, Psalms, and Laments of the Rising Culture* (Ventura, CA: Regal Books, 2007), 31.

8. Matthew the Poor, *Orthodox Prayer Life*, 147.

9. The residential school system was a cultural genocide that stole Indigenous children from their families in order to "kill the Indian in the child." Children were taken from their families at the age of five years old and were systematically forced to abandon their culture. Their language was forbidden, their braids were cut off, their history was suppressed. This also created the environment for widespread physical and sexual abuse. These schools were implemented by the government and church beginning in the 1830s. The last one closed in 1996.

Chapter 5 Contented Community

1. Wendell Berry, *The Unsettling of America: Culture and Agriculture* (San Francisco: Sierra Club Books, 1977), 24.

2. William Barclay, *The Gospel of Matthew*, vol. 2 (Louisville: Westminster John Knox, 2001), 111.

3. "A Covenant Prayer in the Wesleyan Tradition," *The United Methodist Hymnal*, #607, http://geneseoumc.org/wp-content/uploads/2011/03/Wesley-Covenant.pdf.

4. Berry, *Unsettling of America*, 14.

5. Thomas Merton, *No Man Is an Island* (Boston: Shambala, 2005), 137.

6. Reinhold Niebuhr, quoted in Elisabeth Sifton, *The Serenity Prayer: Faith and Politics in Times of Peace and War* (New York: Norton, 2003), 277.

7. "Oceti Sakowin," Stand with Standing Rock, http://standwithstandingrock.net /oceti-sakowin.

8. "Camp Etiquette," Stand with Standing Rock, https://standwithstandingrock
.net/camp-etiquette.

9. *Cape-Colored* is a term referring to a distinct ethnic group in South Africa whose
diverse ancestry includes Indigenous Khoisan and Xhosa people as well as European
colonizers and slaves imported from the Dutch East Indies.

Chapter 6 Ordered Community

1. Gerald G. May, *Addiction and Grace: Love and Spirituality in the Healing of Addictions* (San Francisco: HarperSanFrancisco, 2007), 214.

2. Kathryn Tanner, "Is Capitalism a Belief System?," *Anglican Theological Review* 92,
no. 4 (Fall 2010): 634.

3. David Bentley Hart, "The Pornography Culture," *The New Atlantis*, no. 6 (Summer
2004), https://www.thenewatlantis.com/publications/the-pornography-culture.

4. Alexandr Solzhenitsyn, "A World Split Apart," Commencement Address, Harvard
University, June 8, 1978, Cambridge, MA, *American Rhetoric: Online Speech Bank*, http://
www.americanrhetoric.com/speeches/alexandersolzhenitsynharvard.htm.

5. "20 Mind-Blowing Stats about the Porn Industry and Its Underage Consumers,"
Fight the New Drug, May 30, 2019, https://fightthenewdrug.org/10-porn-stats-that-will
-blow-your-mind.

6. "Pornography Survey," Proven Men, August 28, 2018, https://www.provenmen
.org/wp-content/uploads/2016/09/Survey-eBook-no-links-Linked.pdf.

7. "A Report on the Use of Technology to Recruit, Groom and Sell Domestic Minor Sex
Trafficking Victims," Thorn, January 2015, https://www.thorn.org/wp-content/uploads
/2015/02/Survivor_Survey_r5.pdf.

8. Paul J. Wright, Robert S. Tokunaga, and Ashley Kraus, "A Meta-Analysis of Pornography Consumption and Actual Acts of Sexual Aggression in General Population Studies,"
Journal of Communication 66, no. 1 (February 2016): 183–205.

9. Mary-Lee Bouma, "Porn Use: It's about More than Personal Sin," Do Justice, September 15, 2017, http://dojustice.crcna.org/article/porn-use-its-about-more-personal-sin.

10. Thomas Merton, *New Seeds of Contemplation* (New York: New Directions, 2007), 63.

11. Elder Ephraim, *Counsels from the Holy Mountain: Selected from the Letters and
Homilies of Elder Ephraim* (Florence, AZ: St. Anthony's Greek Orthodox Monastery,
1999), 163.

12. Gerald G. May, *Addiction and Grace: Love and Spirituality in the Healing of Addictions* (San Francisco: HarperSanFrancisco, 2007), 180.

13. Richard C. Goode, "The Calling of Crappy Citizenship: A Plea for Christian Anarchy," *The Other Journal: An Intersection of Theology and Culture* 30 (November 1,
2018), https://theotherjournal.com/2018/11/01/the-calling-of-crappy-citizenship-a-plea
-for-christian-anarchy.

14. Richard Rohr, *Breathing under Water: Spirituality and the Twelve Steps* (Cincinnati:
St. Anthony Messenger, 2011), xx.

15. Karl Barth, quoted in Jan Milič Lochman, "Towards an Ecumenical Account of
Hope," *The Ecumenical Review* 31, no. 1 (January 1979): 18.

16. Annie Dillard, "The Writing Life," *Tikkun Magazine* 3, no. 6 (1988): 24.

17. "Our Vision," Alongsiders International, https://www.alongsiders.org.

18. Andy Gray and Craig Greenfield, *The Alongsiders Story: Equipping One Generation
to Reach the Next* (Cambodia: Alongsiders International, 2017), 46.

Chapter 7 Compassionate Community

1. William Booth, "Original Speech by Salvation Army Founder William Booth," Salvation Army North, YouTube video, June 27, 2016, https://www.youtube.com/watch?v=DK5IqxQmVHs.

2. Brad Jersak, "Our glorification (ascent, theosis), ironically, follows the Way of the Cross (descent, kenosis)," Facebook post, September 18, 2017, https://www.facebook.com/bradley.jersak/posts/10154843437651905.

3. Isaac of Syria, quoted in Shane Claiborne, Jonathan Wilson-Hartgrove, and Enuma Okoro, *Common Prayer: A Liturgy for Ordinary Radicals* (Grand Rapids: Zondervan, 2010), 426.

4. Jean Vanier, *Be Not Afraid* (Toronto: Griffin House, 1975), 21.

5. Gregory of Nyssa, quoted in D. H. Williams, ed., *Matthew: Interpreted by Early Christian Commentators*, The Church's Bible (Grand Rapids: Eerdmans, 2018).

6. John M. Perkins, *Beyond Charity: The Call to Christian Community Development* (Grand Rapids: Baker, 1993), 44.

7. Mark Buchanan, *Your Church Is Too Safe: Why Following Christ Turns the World Upside-Down* (Grand Rapids: Zondervan, 2012), 88–89.

8. Fr. Paul Schroeder, "Building the New City: St. Basil's Social Vision," In Communion, December 7, 2008, https://incommunion.org/2008/12/07/building-the-new-city-st-basils-social-vision.

9. Schroeder, "Building the New City."

10. Schroeder, "Building the New City."

11. *An Unusual Alliance*, directed by Brian MacDonald (Vancouver: V12 Films, 2015), DVD.

Chapter 8 Contemplative Community

1. Gregory of Nyssa, quoted in Shane Claiborne, Jonathan Wilson-Hartgrove, and Enuma Okoro, *Common Prayer: A Liturgy for Ordinary Radicals* (Grand Rapids: Zondervan, 2010), 132.

2. Thomas Merton, quoted in Lawrence S. Cunningham, *Thomas Merton and the Monastic Vision* (Grand Rapids: Eerdmans, 1999), 209.

3. Alexandr Solzhenitsyn, *The Gulag Archipelago* (London: Collins, 1974), 168.

4. Thomas Merton, *Contemplative Prayer* (London: Darton, Longman & Todd, 1973), 26.

5. Merton, *Contemplative Prayer*, 83.

6. Henri J. M. Nouwen, *The Genesee Diary: Report from a Trappist Monastery* (New York: Image, 1989), 76.

7. Abba Isaac the Syrian, quoted in Matthew the Poor, *Orthodox Prayer Life: The Interior Way* (New York: St. Vladimir's Seminary Press, 2003), 210.

8. Kenneth Tanner, "Our Ascension with Christ—Cooperating with Christ in the Renewal of All Things," *Clarion Journal of Spirituality and Justice*, June 7, 2018, http://www.clarion-journal.com/clarion_journal_of_spirit/2018/06/our-ascension-with-christ-cooperating-with-christ-in-the-renewal-of-all-things-kenneth-tanner.html.

9. Wendell Berry, *The Unsettling of America: Culture and Agriculture* (San Francisco: Sierra Club Books, 1977), 98.

10. Annie Dillard, *Pilgrim at Tinker Creek* (New York: Harper Perennial, 2007), 10–11.

11. "Everyday Disciples: John Wesley's 22 Questions," Discipleship Ministries, The United Methodist Church, October 2016, https://www.umcdiscipleship.org/resources/ev eryday-disciples-john-wesleys-22-questions.

Chapter 9 Reconciling Community

1. "Paige's Story: Abuse, Indifference and a Young Life Discarded," Representative for Children and Youth, May 14, 2015, https://rcybc.ca/paige.

2. Christopher C. H. Cook, "Spirituality and Alcohol Dependence," in *Identification and Treatment of Alcohol Dependency*, ed. Colin R. Martin (Keswick, UK: M&K Update, 2008), 295.

3. Mary Anne Muller and Anna Brown, "The Plowshares Eight: Thirty Years On," *Waging Nonviolence*, September 9, 2010, https://wagingnonviolence.org/feature/the-plow shares-8-thirty-years-on.

4. Philip Berrigan, "A Christmas Prayer," Jonah House, http://www.jonahhouse.org /archive/Phil_ChristmasPrayer.htm.

5. Don Pinnock, *Gang Town* (Cape Town, South Africa: Tafelberg, 2016), 155.

6. Travis Lupick, *Fighting for Space: How a Group of Drug Users Transformed One City's Struggle with Addiction* (Vancouver: Arsenal Pulp, 2017), 170.

7. "Faith Action for Children on the Move—Global Partners Forum," General Curia of the Society of Jesus, Rome, Italy, October 16–19, 2018, https://www.wvi.org/sites/default /files/2019-07/Faith-Action-for-Children-on-the-Move-Forum-Report.pdf.

8. Brave Global, http://braveglobal.org.

9. The Truth and Reconciliation Commission of Canada, "Honouring the Truth, Reconciling for the Future: Summary of the Final Report of the Truth and Reconciliation Commission of Canada," 2015, http://nctr.ca/assets/reports/Final%20Reports/Executive _Summary_English_Web.pdf.

Chapter 10 Co-suffering Community

1. Ita Ford, quoted in Shane Claiborne, Jonathan Wilson-Hartgrove, and Enuma Okoro, *Common Prayer: A Liturgy for Ordinary Radicals* (Grand Rapids: Zondervan, 2010), 51.

2. Saint Mark the Ascetic, quoted in Clemens Sedmak, *The Capacity to be Displaced: Resilience, Mission, and Inner Strength* (Leiden: Brill, 2017), 124.

3. Simone Weil, *Waiting for God* (New York: Perennial, 2001), 73.

4. Dan McCartney, quoted in Timothy Keller, *Walking with God through Pain and Suffering* (New York: Dutton, 2013), 152.

5. Charles de Foucauld, quoted in Claiborne, Wilson-Hartgrove, and Okoro, *Common Prayer*, 49.

6. Philip Berrigan, quoted in Christian Piatt, Becky Garrison, Jason Boyett, and Jarrod McKenna, *Banned Questions about the Bible* (St. Louis: Chalice, 2011), 198.

7. James H. Cone, *God of the Oppressed* (Maryknoll, NY: Orbis, 2012), xviii.

8. Weil, *Waiting for God*, 81.

Bibliography

"About Us." San Patrignano. https://www.sanpatrignano.com/about-us.

"Addiction: Our Stupid Friend." *Float House* (blog). https://floathouse.ca/blog-archive /addiction-our-stupid-friend?.

Alcoholics Anonymous: The Story of How Many Thousands of Men and Women Have Recovered from Alcoholism. 4th ed. New York: Alcoholics Anonymous World Services, 2001.

Alexander, Bruce K. "Addiction: Hopeful Prophecy from a Time of Despair." *Bruce K. Alexander* (blog). September 9, 2017. http://www.brucekalexander.com/articles -speeches/dislocation-theory-addiction/290-addiction-a-hopeful-prophecy-from-a -time-of-despair-2.

————. "Healing Addiction through Community: A Much Longer Road Than It Seems?" *Bruce K. Alexander* (blog). May 14, 2015. http://www.brucekalexander.com/articles-s peeches/healing-addiction-through-community-a-much-longer-road-than-it-seems2.

Athanasius. *On the Incarnation.* Translated by John Behr. Yonkers, NY: St. Vladimir's Seminary Press, 2011.

Barclay, William. *The Gospel of Matthew.* Vol. 2. Louisville: Westminster John Knox, 2001.

Berrigan, Philip. "A Christmas Prayer." Jonah House. http://www.jonahhouse.org/archive /Phil_ChristmasPrayer.htm.

Berry, Wendell. *The Unsettling of America: Culture and Agriculture.* San Francisco: Sierra Club Books, 1977.

Booth, William. "Original Speech by Salvation Army Founder William Booth." Salvation Army North. YouTube video. June 27, 2016. https://www.youtube.com/watch?v=D K5IqxQmVHs.

Bouma, Mary-Lee. "Porn Use: It's about More than Personal Sin." Do Justice. September 15, 2017. http://dojustice.crcna.org/article/porn-use-its-about-more-personal-sin.

Boyle, Gregory. *Barking to the Choir: The Power of Radical Kinship.* New York: Simon & Schuster, 2017.

Brand, Russell. *Recovery: Freedom from Our Addictions.* London: Bluebird, 2017.

Brown, Brené. "Everyone Has a Story." *Brené Brown* (blog). June 7, 2018. https://brene brown.com/ blog/2018/06/07/everyone-has-a-story.

Buchanan, Mark. *Your Church Is Too Safe: Why Following Christ Turns the World Upside-Down.* Grand Rapids: Zondervan, 2012.

Buechner, Frederick. *The Sacred Journey: A Memoir of Early Days.* San Francisco: Harper & Row, 1982.

Campbell, Larry, Neil Boyd, and Lori Culbert. *A Thousand Dreams: Vancouver's Downtown Eastside and the Fight for Its Future.* Vancouver: Greystone Books, 2009.

Catherine of Genoa. "Life and Teachings." In *Devotional Classics,* edited by Richard Foster and James Bryan Smith, 212–17. San Francisco: HarperSanFrancisco, 1990.

Claiborne, Shane, Jonathan Wilson-Hartgrove, and Enuma Okoro. *Common Prayer: A Liturgy for Ordinary Radicals.* Grand Rapids: Zondervan, 2010.

Cone, James H. *God of the Oppressed.* Maryknoll, NY: Orbis, 2012.

Cook, Christopher C. H. "Spirituality and Alcohol Dependence." In *Identification and Treatment of Alcohol Dependency,* edited by Colin R. Martin, 289–302. Keswick, UK: M&K Update, 2008.

"A Covenant Prayer in the Wesleyan Tradition." *The United Methodist Hymnal,* #607. htt p://geneseoumc.org/wp-content/uploads/2011/03/Wesley-Covenant.pdf.

Crosby, Michael H. *Spirituality of the Beatitudes: Matthew's Challenge for First World Christians.* Maryknoll, NY: Orbis, 1980.

Cunningham, Lawrence S. *Thomas Merton and the Monastic Vision.* Grand Rapids: Eerdmans, 1999.

Dart, Ron. "The Beatitudes (Matthew 5:3–12)—Translation by Ron Dart." *Clarion Journal of Spirituality and Justice.* February 5, 2018. http://www.clarion-journal.com/clarion _journal_of_spirit/2018/02/the-beatitudes-matthew-53-12-translation-by-ron-dart.html.

Day, Dorothy. *The Long Loneliness.* San Francisco: HarperSanFrancisco, 1981.

de Waal, Esther. *Seeking God: The Way of St. Benedict.* Collegeville, MN: Liturgical Press, 2001.

Dillard, Annie. *Pilgrim at Tinker Creek.* New York: Harper Perennial, 2007.

———. "The Writing Life." *Tikkun Magazine* 3, no. 6 (1988): 24–27.

Dykstra, Laurel. *Set Them Free: The Other Side of Exodus.* Maryknoll, NY: Orbis, 2002.

Ekblad, Bob. *The Beautiful Gate: Enter Jesus' Global Liberation Movement.* Burlington, WA: People's Seminary, 2017.

Eklund, Rebekah. "Blessed Are the Image-Bearers: Gregory of Nyssa and the Beatitudes." *Anglican Theological Review* 99, no. 4 (Fall 2017): 729–40.

Ephraim, Elder. *Counsels from the Holy Mountain: Selected from the Letters and Homilies of Elder Ephraim.* Florence, AZ: St. Anthony's Greek Orthodox Monastery, 1999.

"Faith Action for Children on the Move—Global Partners Forum." General Curia of the Society of Jesus, Rome, Italy, October 16–19, 2018. https://www.wvi.org/sites/default /files/2019-07/Faith-Action-for-Children-on-the-Move-Forum-Report.pdf.

Finlan, Stephen, and Vladimir Kharlamov, eds. *Theosis: Deification in Christian Theology.* Eugene, OR: Pickwick, 2006.

Forest, Jim. "Climbing the Ladder of the Beatitudes." *Jim and Nancy Forest* (blog). August 16, 2017. http://jimandnancyforest.com/2017/08/climbing-the-ladder-of-the-beatitudes.

Foster, Richard J. *Celebration of Discipline: The Path to Spiritual Growth*. Rev. ed. New York: HarperCollins, 1998.

Frankl, Viktor E. *Psychotherapy and Existentialism: Selected Papers on Logotherapy*. New York: Pocket Books, 1967.

Garland, David E. *Reading Matthew: A Literary and Theological Commentary*. Macon, GA: Smyth & Helwys, 2001.

Gbowee, Leymah, and Carol Mithers. *Mighty Be Our Powers: How Sisterhood, Prayer, and Sex Changed a Nation at War*. New York: Beast Books, 2011.

Glerup, Michael. *Gregory of Nyssa: Sermons on the Beatitudes*. Classics in Spiritual Formation. Downers Grove, IL: InterVarsity, 2012.

Goode, Richard C. "The Calling of Crappy Citizenship: A Plea for Christian Anarchy." *The Other Journal: An Intersection of Theology and Culture* 30 (November 1, 2018). https://theotherjournal.com/2018/11/01/the-calling-of-crappy-citizenship-a-plea-for-christian-anarchy.

Gray, Andy, and Craig Greenfield. *The Alongsiders Story: Equipping One Generation to Reach the Next*. Cambodia: Alongsiders International, 2017.

Gregory of Nyssa. *The Life of Moses*. The Classics of Western Spirituality Series. Translated by Abraham J. Malherbe and Everett Ferguson. Mahwah, NJ: Paulist Press, 1978.

———. *The Lord's Prayer/The Beatitudes*. Translated by Hilda Graef. Ancient Christian Writers 18. Westminster, MD: Newman, 1954.

Gundry, Robert H. *Matthew: A Commentary on His Handbook for a Mixed Church under Persecution*. Grand Rapids: Eerdmans, 1994.

Hart, David Bentley. "The Pornography Culture." *The New Atlantis*, no. 6 (Summer 2004). https://www.thenewatlantis.com/publications/the-pornography-culture.

Hauerwas, Stanley, and Charles Pinches. *Christians among the Virtues*. Notre Dame, IN: University of Notre Dame Press, 1997.

Heasley, Brian, ed. *Writing on the Wall: Prayers, Psalms, and Laments of the Rising Culture*. Ventura, CA: Regal Books, 2007.

Jersak, Brad. "Our glorification (ascent, theosis), ironically, follows the Way of the Cross (descent, kenosis)." Facebook post. September 18, 2017. https://www.facebook.com/bradley.jersak/posts/10154843437651905.

Keener, Craig S. *A Commentary on the Gospel of Matthew*. Grand Rapids: Eerdmans, 1999.

Keller, Timothy. *Walking with God through Pain and Suffering*. New York: Dutton, 2013.

Kilby, Karen. "Perichoresis and Projection: Problems with Social Doctrines of the Trinity." *New Blackfriars* 81 (November 2000): 432–45.

Le Guin, Ursula K. *The Dispossessed*. New York: Eos, 2001.

Levine, Amy-Jill. "Matthew's Advice to a Divided Readership." In *The Gospel of Matthew in Current Study*, edited by David E. Aune, 22–41. Grand Rapids: Eerdmans, 2001.

Lewis, C. S. *Mere Christianity*. New York: Macmillan, 1977.

Little, Simon. "Hallucinogen That Heals? One B.C. Psychotherapist's Experience with Ayahuasca." *Global News*, April 25, 2018. https://globalnews.ca/news/4166406/aya huasca-mental-health-addiction.

Lochman, Jan Milič. "Towards an Ecumenical Account of Hope." *The Ecumenical Review* 31, no. 1 (January 1979): 13–30.

Lupick, Travis. *Fighting for Space: How a Group of Drug Users Transformed One City's Struggle with Addiction.* Vancouver: Arsenal Pulp, 2017.

———. "Vancouver City Council Told Fentanyl Meant 2017 Saw a Record Number of Drug-Overdose Deaths." *Georgia Straight.* January 17, 2018. https://www.straight.com/news/1020446/vancouver-city-council-told-fentanyl-meant-2017-saw-record-number-drug-overdose-deaths.

MacDonald, Brian, dir. *An Unusual Alliance.* DVD. 2015; Vancouver, Canada: V12Films.com.

Maté, Gabor. *In the Realm of Hungry Ghosts: Close Encounters with Addiction.* Toronto: Vintage Canada, 2012.

Matthew the Poor. *Orthodox Prayer Life: The Interior Way.* New York: St. Vladimir's Seminary Press, 2003.

May, Gerald G. *Addiction and Grace: Love and Spirituality in the Healing of Addictions.* San Francisco: HarperSanFrancisco, 2007.

McGrath, Alister E. *Christian Theology: An Introduction.* Oxford: Oxford University Press, 1997.

Merton, Thomas. *Contemplative Prayer.* London: Darton, Longman & Todd, 1973.

———. *New Seeds of Contemplation.* New York: New Directions, 2007.

———. *No Man Is an Island.* Boston: Shambala, 2005.

———. *Thoughts in Solitude.* New York: Farrar, Straus and Cudahy, 1958.

Milbank, John, Graham Ward, and Edith Wyschogrod. *Theological Perspectives on God and Beauty.* Harrisburg, PA: Trinity Press International, 2003.

Muller, Mary Anne, and Anna Brown. "The Plowshares Eight: Thirty Years On." *Waging Nonviolence.* September 9, 2010. https://wagingnonviolence.org/feature/the-plowshares-8-thirty-years-on.

Nguyen, Viet Thanh, ed. *The Displaced: Refugee Writers on Refugee Lives.* New York: Abrams, 2018.

Nouwen, Henri J. M. *The Genesee Diary: Report from a Trappist Monastery.* New York: Image, 1989.

———. *The Road to Daybreak: A Spiritual Journey.* New York: Image, 1990.

O'Day, Gail R. "Surprised by Faith: Jesus and the Canaanite Woman." In *A Feminist Companion to Matthew,* edited by Amy-Jill Levine, 114–25. Sheffield, UK: Sheffield Academic Press, 2001.

O'Rourke, Meghan. "Good Grief: Is There a Better Way to Be Bereaved?" *New Yorker,* February 1, 2010. https://www.newyorker.com/magazine/2010/02/01/good-grief.

Osborn, Bud. *Hundred Block Rock.* Vancouver: Arsenal Pulp, 1999.

"Our Vision." Alongsiders International. https://www.alongsiders.org.

"Paige's Story: Abuse, Indifference and a Young Life Discarded." Representative for Children and Youth. May 14, 2015. https://rcybc.ca/paige.

Pearson, Caryn, Teresa Janz, and Jennifer Ali. "Mental and Substance Use Disorders in Canada." Statistics Canada. Last modified November 27, 2015. http://www.statcan .gc.ca/pub/82-624-x/2013001/article/11855-eng.htm.

Perkins, John M. *Beyond Charity: The Call to Christian Community Development*. Grand Rapids: Baker, 1993.

Petcu, Liviu. "The Doctrine of Epektasis. One of the Major Contributions of Saint Gregory of Nyssa to the History of Thinking." *Revista Portuguesa de Filosofia* 73, no. 2 (2017): 771–82.

Piatt, Christian, Becky Garrison, Jason Boyett, and Jarrod McKenna. *Banned Questions about the Bible*. St. Louis: Chalice, 2011.

Pinnock, Don. *Gang Town*. Cape Town, South Africa: Tafelberg, 2016.

Pullinger, Jacqueline. "Drug Rehabilitation: Transformation through a Reparenting Approach." International Conference on Tackling Drug Abuse, March 5, 2018. https:// www.nd.gov.hk/en/conference_proceedings/Drugs_proBK_Part4/Drugs_proBK _JacqP.pdf.

Rah, Soong-Chan. *Prophetic Lament: A Call for Justice in Troubled Times*. Downers Grove, IL: InterVarsity, 2015.

"A Report on the Use of Technology to Recruit, Groom and Sell Domestic Minor Sex Trafficking Victims." Thorn. January 2015. https://www.thorn.org/wp-content/uploads /2015/02/Survivor_Survey_r5.pdf.

Rohr, Richard. *Breathing under Water: Spirituality and the Twelve Steps*. Cincinnati: St. Anthony Messenger, 2011.

Romero, Oscar. *The Violence of Love*. Maryknoll, NY: Orbis, 2004.

Rothfuss, Patrick. *The Name of the Wind*. New York: Daw Books, 2007.

Schroeder, Fr. Paul. "Building the New City: St. Basil's Social Vision." In Communion, December 7, 2008. https://incommunion.org/2008/12/07/building-the-new-city-st-basils -social-vision.

Sedmak, Clemens. *The Capacity to Be Displaced: Resilience, Mission, and Inner Strength*. Leiden: Brill, 2017.

Sifton, Elisabeth. *The Serenity Prayer: Faith and Politics in Times of Peace and War*. New York: Norton, 2003.

Smith, Glenn. "Reading Your Community: Towards an Authentic Encounter with the City." https://churchforvancouver.ca/reading-your-community-towards-an-authent ic-encounter-with-the-city.

Solzhenitsyn, Alexandr. *The Gulag Archipelago*. London: Collins, 1974.

———. "A World Split Apart." Commencement Address. Harvard University, June 8, 1978, Cambridge, MA. *American Rhetoric: Online Speech Bank*. http://www.americ anrhetoric.com/speeches/alexandersolzhenitsynharvard.htm.

Stapleton, Chris, and Lee Thomas Miller. "Whiskey and You." Track 5 on Chris Stapleton, *Traveller*. Mercury Nashville, 2015.

"Statistics on Addiction in America." Addiction Center, July 15, 2019. https://www .addictioncenter.com/addiction/addiction-statistics.

Tanner, Kathryn. "Is Capitalism a Belief System?" *Anglican Theological Review* 92, no. 4 (Fall 2010): 617–36.

Tanner, Kenneth. "Our Ascension with Christ—Cooperating with Christ in the Renewal of All Things." *Clarion Journal of Spirituality and Justice*, June 7, 2018. http://www .clarion-journal.com/clarion_journal_of_spirit/2018/06/our-ascension-with-christ-co operating-with-christ-in-the-renewal-of-all-things-kenneth-tanner.html.

Taylor, Charles. *Sources of the Self: The Making of the Modern Identity*. Cambridge, MA: Harvard University Press, 1989.

Toews, Miriam. *All My Puny Sorrows*. New York: Knopf, 2014.

The Truth and Reconciliation Commission of Canada. "Honouring the Truth, Reconciling for the Future: Summary of the Final Report of the Truth and Reconciliation Commission of Canada," 2015. http://nctr.ca/assets/reports/Final%20Reports/Exec utive_Summary_English_Web.pdf.

"20 Mind-Blowing Stats about the Porn Industry and Its Underage Consumers." Fight the New Drug. May 30, 2019. https://fightthenewdrug.org/10-porn-stats-that-will-b low-your-mind.

Vanier, Jean. *Be Not Afraid*. Toronto: Griffin House, 1975.

———. *From Brokenness to Community*. Mahwah, NJ: Paulist Press, 1992.

Weil, Simone. *Waiting for God*. New York: Perennial, 2001.

West, Cornel, and Christa Buschendorf. *Black Prophetic Fire*. Boston: Beacon, 2014.

Willard, Dallas. *The Divine Conspiracy: Rediscovering Our Hidden Life in God*. San Francisco: HarperSanFrancisco, 1998.

———. *The Spirit of the Disciplines: Understanding How God Changes Lives*. San Francisco: HarperSanFrancisco, 1991.

Williams, D. H., ed. *Matthew: Interpreted by Early Christian Commentators*. The Church's Bible. Grand Rapids: Eerdmans, 2018.

Wilson, Charles R. "Christology: The Incarnate Word of God." In *A Contemporary Wesleyan Theology: Biblical, Systematic, and Practical*. Vol. 1. Edited by Charles W. Carter, 331–69. Grand Rapids: Asbury Press, 1983.

Wright, N. T. *Jesus and the Victory of God*. Christian Origins and the Question of God. Vol. 2. London: SPCK, 1999.

Wright, Paul J., Robert S. Tokunaga, and Ashley Kraus. "A Meta-Analysis of Pornography Consumption and Actual Acts of Sexual Aggression in General Population Studies." *Journal of Communication* 66, no. 1 (February 2016): 183–205.

Yong, Ed. "A Landmark Study on the Origins of Alcoholism." *The Atlantic*. June 21, 2018. https://www.theatlantic.com/science/archive/2018/06/a-landmark-study-in-the -origins-of-alcoholism/563372.

Index

Lightning Source UK Ltd.
Milton Keynes UK
UKHW021924071022
410079UK00011B/692